Feeling Loved:
Connecting with God
In the Minutes You Have

Feeling Loved:
Connecting with God
In the Minutes You Have

Marnie Swedberg

The Marnie Method Series for Super Busy Women
Visit http://www.Marnie.com

Book I. **The Marnie Method**
Series for Super Busy Women.

Feeling Loved:
Connecting with God
In the Minutes You Have

Copyright 2010
by **Marnie Swedberg**
http://www.Marnie.com

Cover Design by
Paul Archie Teleron

Layout Design by
Carlos Eluterio Estrada
& Surendra Gupta

Cover Quotes from

Karyn Brinkmeyer
www.KarynBrinkmeyer.com

Shannon Ethridge
www.shannonethridge.com

Gail Gaymer Martin
www.GailMartin.com.

Jill Savage
www.JillSavage.com

Pam Farrel
www.PamandBill.org.

Unless otherwise noted, Scripture notations are from the Amplified Bible, (AMP), Grand Rapids, MI: Zondervan Bible, 1983. Verses marked KJV are from the King James Version, Oxford Univ Pr, 2010. Scripture quotations marked NASB are from the New American Standard Bible, [Nashville, Tenn.]: Nelson Bibles, 2006. Scripture quotations marked NIV are taken from the New International Version. Grand Rapids, MI: Zondervan, 2005. Verses marked NKJV are taken from the Holy Bible New King James Version, Casscom Media, 2003, and Scripture quotations marked NLT are taken from the New Living Translation, Carol Stream, IL: Tyndale House, 2009.

All rights reserved.
Published in the United States of America.

No part of this book may be used or reproduced in any manner whatsoever without written permission except in the case of brief quotations embodied in critical articles and reviews.

For more information contact:
Gifts of Encouragement, Inc.
375 N. Stephanie St., Suite 1411
Henderson, NV 89014
877-77-HOW-TO
Info@Marnie.com
http://www.Marnie.com.

    Swedberg, Marnie.
        Feeling Loved: Connecting with God in the Minutes You Have/by Marnie Swedberg
           p.   cm.

ISBN 978-0-9829935-0-7
1. Christian Life.   2. Inspiration.   3. Worship & Devotion.   I. Title: Feeling Loved

First Edition/Book: 2010

Table of Contents

Introduction 1

SECTION I: Feeling Loved 5

CHAPTER 1: God Sees You as "Best Friend" Material 7
CHAPTER 2: The Five Keys to Friendship 15
CHAPTER 3: Gut Honest 21
CHAPTER 4: Humility: The Key to God's Heart 29
CHAPTER 5: Dealing with Feelings 39
CHAPTER 6: Hearing God 45
CHAPTER 7: Affirmations, Meditation & Memorization 53
CHAPTER 8: Praying Scripture 61
CHAPTER 9: Personalities & Prayer 71
CHAPTER 10: Does God Hate Prayer Lists? 81

SECTION II: Scripture Prayers 87

Writing Scripture Prayers 89
1. Prayers of Praise 95
2. Prayers for God's Will To Be Done 103
3. Prayers of Petition 119
4. Prayers of Repentance 125
5. Prayers for Protection 135
6. Prayers of Submission 145

Appendices 155

APPENDIX 1: Jesus is the Bridge to God 157
APPENDIX 2: Questions & Answers 161
APPENDIX 3: Marnie's Top 200 Verses for
Memorization & Meditation 169
APPENDIX 4: Recommended Reading 183

After Words 187

Dedication

This book is dedicated to you if you have ever wanted to feel more of God's love in your life. It's risky business, writing a book like this. It exposes me in ways I'd prefer to avoid. I accept these risks with the hope that something in these pages will help you understand and feel the intensity of the love with which God loves you.

Acknowledgements

Thank you, Dave, Mark, Keren and Tim, for the freedom to pursue my visions and dreams. I love you.

Thank you to my support team at Gifts of Encouragement, Inc., who hail from around the world. I could never do what I do without you.

> Nicole Alarie, Airene Bote, Douglas Brown, Carlos Eluterio Estrada, Surendra Gupta, Ami Krishnamoorthy, Vijay Marathe, Jessica Martinez, Mischa Milano, Romela Moncatar, Tammy Myrick, MC Ramon, Michele Reynolds, Joshua Tallent, Paul Teleron, Katie Deal Wright

Thank you to my volunteer staff and editors. Your willingness to invest into my life and projects affects many others. I am so grateful.

> Kari Anderson, Shirley Brosius, Mary Daniels, Krista Dunk, Gail Dehelain, Lesley Denford, Nicol Eichenberger, Emily Fisher, Nancy Fisher, Vicki Foster, Nancy Kay Grace, Marla Hartson, Susan Helweg, Veronica Klepadlo, Melanie Love, Vicki Mack-Williams, Shobha Massey, Evelyn Mehlhaff, Marcia Mehlhaff, Kim Messinger, Tammy Milbrath, Pat Miller, Comfort Olaleye, Jennifer Richert, Andrea Sharp, Keren Swedberg, Lana Vaughn, Ann Volv

Thank you to our staff at M&K and Soulutions without whose faithful service I would never have time to write books. You are my employees, but also my friends.

> Penny Anderson, Danae Clark, Joanna Heppner, Karen Holmberg-Smith, Lissa Holmberg-Smith, Joel Maxwell, Michelle Maxwell, Hannah Moyer, Mattea Oatman, Theresa Oatman, Rosie Orvis, Kim Ramiller, Natalie Ramiller, Shelbi Rassier, Rylie Scharfenkamp, Laurie Thompson

Thank you to the two editors who saw my potential and fought to see my first book come to publication. "The Marnie Method Series for Super Busy Women" is a direct result of your early belief in me.

> Barbara Anderson, St. Martin's Press and Gwen Weising, Focus on the Family

Thank you to the spiritual and life mentors I mention in this book. Words could never express the impact you each have had on my life.

> Larry Conrad, Karen Fausher, Rev. C. Roger Stacy, Rev. Paul Zoschke

Thank you to all who support me in any way. The list is too long to include here, but please know that I consider myself blessed beyond measure for your participation in my life.

Introduction

Do you feel loved by God?

One day I was sitting with a new friend as she nursed her baby. She was overwhelmed by life and was sharing with me her fears about the future. As she cried, I asked, "Do you ever pray?"

"All the time," she replied without looking up.

"Do you think God hears you?" I queried.

"No," she whispered.

Another day a new neighbor called to ask if her daughter could come over and meet my daughter, Keren. As the girls ran off to play, she and I settled into comfy couches in my living room. It was our first chance to actually talk, although we'd been greeting each other at church for several weeks.

"How long have you been a Christian?" I asked casually.

"I don't think I am one," she replied. "I've always wanted to be one, but I don't know how."

On a different occasion, while sharing a meal with a girlfriend at a local restaurant, my favorite waitress was refilling my water when she said, "We were talking about you last night at church."

I said, "Uh, oh! What about?!"

She matter-of-factly replied, "We were all saying how different you are: Nice, you know. I told them I think it's because you have God in you."

How about you? Have you ever tried to figure out how to connect with God and feel His love?

This book is for all the women who believe there is a God, who love Him and talk to Him the best way they know how, but who still feel disconnected from Him.

If we could spend a few hours together over lunch, I would share some of the concepts I include in this book. It's how I talk. It's how I live.

This is truly a conversational "how to" book instead of one jam-packed with facts and statistics. It is the story of my relationship with God, the feeling of love it generates inside of me and how you can experience God's love in a personal way as well.

There are a few things you might like to know upfront:

- I do not claim to understand everything. God does.
- I fail frequently by letting myself and others down. God is not surprised.
- I weigh over 200 pounds. God sees me as perfect.
- I still beat myself up a bit when I eat without God. God doesn't condemn me.
- I give everyday my best shot. God knows.
- I approach God as a Friend and Savior. God is honored.
- I feel loved by God most of the time. God loves me all of the time.

This is the first book in the Marnie Method series for super busy women because it shares the foundation upon which my life is based and the book series is written.

- I have come to depend on God more than on the air I breathe.
- There is not a day that dawns when God is not on my mind.

- He is the One who wakes me up (not an alarm clock).
- It is God who carries me through each day (not my own strength).
- And it is God who tucks me into bed each night (not sheer exhaustion).

My prayer is that you will come to enjoy a close friendship with God, too. He had a personal friendship with Abraham; He has that kind of friendship with me, and He gave His most precious possession to have that kind of a deep, loving friendship with you.

When a woman tries to love God, yet feels nothing in return, she puts up walls. Like a spurned lover, she can become vindictive and resentful. This separation can lead to despair, but it's completely unnecessary because God truly cares.

My goal here is not to prove that God loves you; that is a fact. My goal is to help you get to know God better so you can come to trust Him and feel His love. Is that what you want?

- Do you want to be closer to God?
- Do you want Him to help you?
- Do you want to know you're OK with Him for ever and ever?
- Do you want to feel like God's love is there for you personally?

If the answer to any of these questions is yes, then let's get going!

Section One

Feeling Loved

Chapter 1
God Sees You as "Best Friend" Material

My Slumber Party with God.

My goal was to pull an all-nighter and I was ready. I had gathered everything I thought I needed to impress and enjoy God into the wee hours of the morning:

- Bible
- Journal
- Pillow
- Blanket
- Boom box
- Cassettes (this ages me, I know!)

My husband, Dave, was traveling and the kids were in bed. As for me, I was psyched up and excited to share a late night date alone with God.

I put in a cassette of worship music and began reading my Bible and journaling my prayers to God. Pretty soon I heard, "click," as the thirty-minute cassette came to its end. I turned it over and began reading and journaling again.

Within a few minutes, another "click."

I changed the cassette once more, trying to repeat the process, but this time I heard the "click" after what felt like only a few seconds.

Baffled, I wondered what was wrong with my player. It was also odd that there were hardly any new words written in my journal.

Then the reality hit me; I was falling asleep.

At first, I was scared!

I mean, it's one thing to fall asleep when having a slumber party with my girlfriends (which, by the way, is what I always do), and Dave can understand when I'm too exhausted for him....

But what happens to someone who is audacious enough to plan a slumber party with God Almighty and then falls asleep in His presence?

It took about two seconds for God to tell me the answer.

In His quiet, gentle way, these truths snuggled into my consciousness:

- He knew I would fall asleep before He accepted the invitation.
- He thought it was "adorable" I wanted to try.
- He was cool with the fact that I might never be able to stay awake into the wee hours with Him in this setting.
- He had fun plans for my future some of which involved middle-of-the-night rendezvous.
- He was not offended in the least. In fact, He was pleased with my desire.

I'll tell you straight: I have come to know for sure that I am one of God's best friends. God treats me like a best friend. Why wouldn't I accept that?

The Marnie Method

Who is Your Best Friend?

I have been blessed with many best friends and each is unique.

- Dave is my life-long, best friend through thick or thin (and believe me, I've been thick).
- My oldest son, Mark, is one of the best listeners and personal coaches I know.
- My daughter, Keren, is one of the most talented, fun and beautiful best friends I have.
- My youngest son, Timothy, is the life of my party.
- My sister, Vicki, is the only person in the world who can read my mind from thousands of miles away.
- My friend, Nancy, predicts my needs and organizes support before I even recognize I'm in trouble.
- My mentor, Karen Fausher, actually hiked through a blizzard to make me chicken noodle soup when I was pregnant, sick and home alone.

I could list dozens of additional best friends, all of whom have this uncanny ability to know what makes me tick, what ticks me off and what turns my crank.

A best friend knows you, sees your weaknesses and loves you still.

God Behaves Like a Best Friend.

My mom loves to tell the story about the time her best friend, God, answered a prayer before she even prayed it.

My father had gone through triple bypass surgery. Early in his recovery, his lungs began filling with fluid. The doctor drilled a hole under his arm, into which they put a drain. In the process a nerve was struck and the pain was excruciating. No amount of pain control was touching it; Dad was beside himself.

After being as helpful as she could for a long time, Mom was overcome with exhaustion. She remembers crossing her arms on Dad's bed, laying her head down and breathing up this prayer, "God, if Harry and Janet could come, it would help." Then she fell asleep.

Harry was Dad's oldest brother from a different city, scheduled to arrive in two days.

Mom says, "I think God knocked us both out, because when I woke up a bit later, Kenny (my dad) was beginning to wake up, too." At that very moment, Harry and his wife, Janet, came walking into Dad's hospital room.

Janet later shared how they were planning to come on Wednesday, but early that morning Harry came out and said, "I think we should go up to see Kenny today. Can you hurry and get ready right now?" Thus began the five-hour drive, two days early.

Mom loves this story not only because God directly answered her prayer, but because He began to answer it hours before she knew she needed to ask.

My mom's friends tease her about all the wonderful "coincidences" that happen in her life. She gives credit to God. As William Temple once said, "When I pray, coincidences happen, and when I don't pray, they don't." [1]

Every day God continues to provide fresh evidence of His care for His friends. Just this morning my restaurant manager, Kim, who is a personal friend of God, told me the true story of how He allowed her to show His love to another one of His best friends.

While attending her grandmother's funeral, Kim had the chance to meet a gal who had recently married into the clan and was being submerged into her new extended family, all at once.

After the long drive home, Kim promptly wrote a note letting her know how much they all loved meeting her, and how perfectly she fit into the family. Although the letter was in her purse, addressed and ready to mail, she realized the postal service between the U.S. and Canada was often slow. She decided to call instead.

As the conversation progressed, Kim expressed many thoughts, including a specific comment about what a perfect match she was for their family.

> "A best friend knows you, sees your weaknesses and loves you still."

After hearing Kim's words of encouragement, she burst into tears and said, "I was doing my devotions right now and asked God if I could have some type of confirmation that I fit in. I can't believe it. I barely had time to pray for this, and here you are calling me."

Kim knew nothing of her need for encouragement or her prayer, but God did. He arranged their long distance connection at exactly the right time.

Talk to God Like You Talk to a Friend.

God is in heaven, but He is also close by. If you've invited Him into your life, using Jesus as the bridge, then He is actually inside you. (If you aren't aware that Jesus is the bridge, see Appendix 1.)

Don't talk to Him as if He's far away. Talk with God as if you know for sure that He's present with you right here.

I carry on conversations with God in practically the same way I do with all the other important people in my life, with these humorous differences:

1. **He isn't a big talker.** I'm from a family of all girls. My sisters and I tease around that God must be a man--because He doesn't chatter on like we do.
2. **He doesn't talk out loud ... hardly ever.** I've never heard Him speak in an audible voice, yet I hear from Him all the time
3. **He is sometimes incomprehensible.** He's huge. He makes Himself small for our sakes, in order to befriend us, but we must never forget that He is, in fact, God.

In His own perfect way, God is very communicative. I hear from Him in a thousand ways including:

- Sunrises and sunsets; the stars, trees, flowers
- Rainfalls and rainbows; billowing clouds and clear skies
- Songs on the radio, with the love messages I need to hear from Him
- Sermons or books, articles or stories that answer my most burning questions
- Hugs in person, online, on my phone or in the mail
- Helping hands in my times of need
- Verses from the Bible that seem to jump off the page at me
- Gentle whispers, as God breathes His love into my conscious mind

So why do we often feel like God is silent?

There is actually only one thing that can make us feel separated from the love of God and it isn't something God is doing.

It is a choice we make. We must choose to either ignore Him or accept Him.

In the same way as we become best friends with another human, we can become best friends with God. But God doesn't force Himself on us. He invites us to draw near to Him. He extends thousands of invitations but leaves the decision up to us.

Conversation Starters.

1. Do you have a best friend? What is it that makes this person so special to you?
2. If you planned a "date" with God, would you plan a slumber-party or what?
3. Do you hear from God? Is there a time you can point to when God answered a specific prayer for you? How about a time when He answered even before you asked?
4. Has God ever chosen you to be someone else's answer to prayer? How did that feel? Or, if you didn't act on His promptings, how did that feel?

End Notes.

1. http://quotationsbook.com/quote/31995/

Chapter 2
The Five Keys to Friendship

When we were newly married, Dave and I moved 300 miles away from Minneapolis where I grew up, to Grand Forks, North Dakota where he had found a job. Even though I was in love and he was my best friend, I had never lived in a city without my parents and sisters, and I was lonely. There were some nights when I even cried myself to sleep.

The people in Grand Forks were friendly and accepting, but it still took over a year for me to meet a best friend.

The first day Joan and I planned an outing, we ended up spending four hours together. We laughed and talked as if we'd always known each other. Dave became good friends with Joan's husband, Lynn, and we double dated almost every week. The guys built their dream aquariums, we all went camping together; life was good.

A few years later, Lynn and Joan moved west and we moved east.

We didn't see each other for over ten years. When we got together again, it was as if no time had elapsed. It's been ten more years since then, but even thinking of Joan makes me smile.

Being together in person isn't everything, but admittedly, it makes developing a friendship easier. Conversely, we don't become best friends with every person with whom we spend a lot of time. We choose our best friends.

- Not every person chooses to be best friends with God.
- God, for His part, extends a deep level of intimacy to everyone who wants it.

If you desire a close, personal friendship with God, go for it, because He has been waiting for you.

The following are some simple ways to begin "feeling" the love God has always been extending in your direction.

1. Spend Time Together.

After going through her first 12-week Bible study, I asked one of the new participants what she thought of it. She said, "I liked it. I feel like I'm starting to get to know Jesus, and that's good. Because it's hard to love someone you hardly know."

Spending time with another person is one of the best ways to get closer to them.

Many friendships can survive time-deprivation, but usually only those whose beginnings involved an intense amount of time investment. Even couples who commit to each other for life, through marriage, have difficulty hanging together over the course of time if not solidly grounded in their love relationship before an extended separation.

If you want to become best friends with God, you will have to spend time with Him and this book shares how I do it.

2. Learn Each Other's History.

Dave and I recently celebrated our 27th anniversary and I am still hearing stories from his pre-Marnie days. Last week he told me about his move to Seattle, Washington, where he knew no one, but was able to find a single room to rent in the back of a granite shop. It was a small room with a cot. He hadn't noticed anything else about the place until his first night alone in the building. In the middle of the night he awoke to realize he was alone, on a cot, in a strange city with a graveyard right outside his window. Eeeooow!

> "Spending time with another person is one of the best ways to get closer to them."

Getting to know someone includes getting to know their history. The Bible is the book of God's history. It is HIS-story, which is why so many God-lovers spend hours on end reading, studying and even memorizing that book.

The Bible is the ultimate love letter from God to you.

God is so much more than a historical figure, but exploring HIStory can help you understand Him better, trust Him more and recognize His never-ending love for you.

Spending time reading and studying the stories in the Bible is one of the most rewarding pastimes I enjoy.

How do you spend your free minutes? Next time you see even ten spare minutes, why not read the Bible and ask God to help you understand it from His perspective?

3. Invest.

Rev. C. Roger Stacy, "Roger," was my youth pastor and the one who performed the wedding ceremony for Dave and me. He is still a good friend and mentor.

In one of my all-time favorite messages he said, "If you don't love something enough, invest more."

The antidote for indifference or alienation in marriages, ministries, parenting or anything else is simply to invest more. If you want a better marriage, choose to spend more time, money or emotion on it. If you feel distant from your children, spend more time, money or emotion on them. If you want to feel closer to God, invest yourself in His direction.

The reality is that God has been thinking about you and investing in you since before you were born. Psalm 139 expresses it well.

- **God created you.** "For you created my inmost being; you knit me together in my mother's womb. When I was made in the secret place, when I was woven together in the depths of the earth, your eyes saw my unformed body."
- **God thinks about you constantly.** "How precious to me are your thoughts, oh God. How vast is the sum of them! Were I to count them, they would outnumber the grains of sand."
- **He knows every word you have said and everything you have yet to say.** "Before a word is on my tongue you know it completely, oh Lord."
- **He knows how long you'll live.** "All the days ordained for me were written in your book before one of them came to be."

God has invested more into your life than any other person. He knows you best and loves you most.

If you're like me, you'll come to appreciate every free minute you have as an opportunity to invest in your relationship with God.

4. Discover Character Qualities, Gifts and Strengths.

God already knows everything there is to know about you. In fact, He knows more about you than you know about yourself, right down to the number of hairs on your head.

You, on the other hand, have to learn about God's qualities, characteristics and gifts one at a time.

I have found this part of my relationship with God to be the delight of my life; sort of like the dating years, it's comprised of one fascinating discovery after another, often in rapid succession.

A few years ago I wrote a song about it[1]. The chorus goes like this:

> I will seek You, Lord, as silver,
> I will search for You as gold;
> Hidden treasure, buried jewels,
> Riches untold.
> If I tire in my search for You,
> Please keep my spirit true,
> For gold and silver, hidden jewels,
> Lord, for precious You!

It "feels" easier to ignore God and stay preoccupied with our busy lives. It takes commitment to push past our habitual neglect of Him.

5. Love Despite Weaknesses and Shortcomings.

God is sometimes hard to love despite the fact He has no weaknesses or shortcomings. When life seems most unfair, I can get pretty mad at Him. Strong negative emotions toward God are not foreign to me.

The prophet Isaiah quotes God as saying, "My thoughts are not your thoughts, neither are your ways My ways," declares the Lord. "As the heavens are higher than the earth, so are My ways higher than your ways and My thoughts than your thoughts." (Isaiah 55:8-9)

It takes faith to look past God's bigness and trust His love for me, just as I am.

For His part, God is fully aware of my sins and failures. As Joyce Meyer likes to say, "He knew what He was getting when He got me!"

Other friends may come and go, but God knows all about you in advance and has committed Himself to loving you--even before you were born.

Conversation Starters.

1. How does it make you feel to know God has been looking forward to becoming best friends with you?
2. How would you describe your friendship with God right now? What choices have led you here? Is this how you want it to stay?
3. People have invested into our lives, obviously. God's investments can be far less obvious. In what ways can you identify God's investment into your life?
4. To what degree are you ready to commit your life to Him today?

End Notes.

1. Swedberg, Marnie. I Will Seek You. 2000. Song. http://www.Marnie.com/songs.php, USA.

Chapter 3
Gut Honest

Years ago my son, Timmy, was snuggling on my lap. After a time, he pushed back, took my chin in his hands and whispered toward my mouth (the way small children do before they realize we hear with our ears):

> "Mommy, I love you so much!
> Sometimes I hate you,
> but mostly I love you!"

What a picture of childlike faith. He was so honest! He trusted me to love him and proved it by expressing his true feelings. My first reaction was surprise followed by intensified love for the little guy.

I, too, experience mixed feelings toward every person with whom I am in a relationship; my husband, my children, my friends, and yes, even with God. This humorous, candid moment between my son and me helped me understand why God always calls King David his favorite. In the Psalms, King David vented

> "God loves it when we are vulnerable with Him."

his raw emotions toward God on a regular basis. He did it respectfully, but he did it, and God loved it!

We all say integrity is important in our relationships, yet mostly we hide our true selves. We put our best foot forward, dress for success and cover-up with Cover Girl®.

Hiding our flaws seems noble and is highly valued in our society. But if we try to hide our flaws from God, it stifles the relationship to the point where we can no longer feel His love.

The beauty (and terror) of developing a relationship with God is that He already knows everything. What's done in Vegas, is seen in heaven. There is absolutely no way to hide anything from God.

> "What's done in Vegas is seen in heaven."

One of the greatest challenges to feeling loved by God is our own desire to camouflage our weaknesses. Are you willing to be vulnerable enough to admit that He already knows everything?

Are You Mad at God?

Does it make you mad that God gets to be in control? Does it irritate you that He knows everything about your past? Do you wish there was a place you might hide from Him, even for a few minutes?

Sometimes I feel very strong, negative emotions toward God including anger, hurt or even hate. He is the perfect one, not me. I sometimes feel resentful of how He works, what He allows and what He chooses to withhold from me, even when I say please.

Emotions, including love and hate, can flash through my mind as quickly as lightning strikes from a cloud-filled sky. In an instant, things can go from sunny to partly overcast, and a moment later to sizzling, with little or no warning.

God loves it when we are vulnerable with Him. He wants us to share everything--even our most negative, embarrassing and painful feelings.

We tend to hide the volatility. We are used to dealing with people and most cannot handle our strong emotions.

We seem to think it's inappropriate or disrespectful to be real with God, or to feel anything less than Pollyanna-like about Him.

> "Emotions are meant to draw us toward God, not away from Him."

The truth is the exact opposite. God hates our attempts to hide ourselves from Him because He knows it leads to unnecessary pain.

The Bible talks a lot about people who pretend; it calls them Pharisees. I love this definition: "A Pharisee is one who wants to get the right formula and do it right and fix everything and feel very wonderful."[1]

That describes me! Can you relate?

If you are ready to quit lying to God about your true feelings, then fill in the blanks below with things about God that have been bothering you for a long time. It's part of getting closer to God--this willingness to admit He already knows it all.

He created our emotions to serve a purpose; emotions are meant to draw us toward God, not away from Him. See if you can fill in the blank:

"I am upset with God because _____.
Or, maybe yours should read, "I feel hurt that God allowed _____.

Being as transparent as you can, are you able to think of even one thing? If you can't do it yet, that's okay. This page will be right here waiting for you, when you're ready.

Digging Deeper.

Beyond admitting our own faults and failures, and "fessing-up" to the fact that we might resent God for being God, we've got a few other road blocks standing between us and our ability to feel His love.

Do this little project with me.

Pretend I'm an old-fashioned psychiatrist and you're on the couch. Let your mind go blank and then answer the following question with whatever words come to mind first.

Do not allow yourself to negate any thought that pops up. Rather, tell God exactly what comes into your mind. Here is the question: What reasons do you have for not trusting God with every fiber of your being? Rephrased, why are you rejecting God's involvement in even the smallest detail of your life?

Pause right now and answer. Tell your answer to God.

Same drill with another question. Why do you think God owes you anything, including the things that came to mind a moment ago?

Clarifying Question.

Is it possible that God, from His vantage point of viewing all of eternity at once, might know something about the past, present or future that gives Him a different perspective about the set of circumstances that are so hurtful in your memory? Is this even a possibility?

☐ Yes   ☐ No   ☐ Maybe   ☐ I think this is a trick question.

Giving God the Benefit of the Doubt.

Every time I've battled through to the root source of an intense pain in my own experience, I have found a loving God waiting for me at the bottom of it.

I'm not saying God is the cause of every pain, but rather that I've learned He waits for us to come to Him from wherever we are--and often we find ourselves very low, like the saying, "I hit the bottom of the barrel." You know, times when life is so hard that we exhaust our ability to solve, fix or move past the pain.

I believe God sits at the bottom of the barrels of life, waiting for us to finally notice Him, share our true feelings with Him and trust Him.

When the bottom of the barrel falls out, and you find yourself free-falling emotionally, God is there, too, even when it's your own fault. He is waiting for your call so He can cushion your fall.

The goal is to more quickly invite God's participation in getting us out of deep, dark emotional pits. One trick is to give God the opportunity to bring good out of bad. Here are some common, everyday examples of how these look in my life:

- Missed an appointment due to weather or an employee's illness? Maybe I would have made a decision I would later regret. Maybe there is someone in my new path for me to encourage.
- No compassion for me due to someone else's busy schedule or personal pain? Maybe God wants to spend some extra quality time with me today, comforting me directly.
- No Internet connection this afternoon? Maybe there is something else I am supposed to be doing with these hours.

It takes practice to consistently give God the benefit of the doubt, but it's worth the investment. As we learn to run our emotions to Him, recognizing them, capturing them and bringing them into the safe-haven of God's realm, we get faster and faster at it.

- If a "bad guy" was chasing a sprinter, he'd have a much harder time catching her than if he was chasing a non-athlete.
- If a debilitating emotion is chasing you, you need to be able to run it quickly to Jesus, before it overwhelms you.

It takes training. It doesn't just happen. The distance between our awareness of trauma and our conscious connection with Jesus needs to get shorter every day, every week and every year.

There is an old hymn that sounds strange now, but says it best. Read the words with the understanding that we are "Gilead" and Jesus is "the balm."

> There is a balm in Gilead,
> To make the wounded whole;
> There is a balm in Gilead,
> To heal the sin-sick soul.
>
> Sometimes I feel discouraged,
> And think my work's in vain,
> But then the Holy Spirit,
> Revives my soul again.
>
> If you cannot preach like Peter,
> If you cannot pray like Paul,
> You can tell the love of Jesus
> And say, "He died for all."[2]

My own rendition of this reality is as follows:

> We are the sobbing child.
> Jesus is the comforting mother.
>
> We are the bleeding patient.
> Jesus is the healing physician.
>
> We are the lonely partner.
> Jesus is the Lover of our souls.
>
> We are inadequate.
> Jesus is our adequacy.

Jesus lived a perfect life then laid down His life on the cross so we could access God directly through Him. Hebrews 7:25 says it this way, "Therefore [Jesus] is able to save completely those who come to God through Him, because He always lives to intercede for them."

Like a passenger who has fallen off a ship and is moving quickly away from the safety of its decks, self-absorption carries us away from feeling God's love. Jesus is like a life preserver, thrown out to save us. We have a choice--reach out to Him or pretend we aren't in trouble.

Conversation Starters.

1. What emotions have carried you away from God when you needed Him most?
2. Do you feel you can be genuinely honest with God? Why or why not?
3. Do you have any "Vegas" memories you are willing to give to God right now?

End Notes.

1. Prevallet, Elaine M. "Dancing Around the Kingdom: Notes from an Occasional Journal." Weavings Jan/Feb 1995: 32.
2. Traditional Spiritual. There is a Balm in Gilead. Undated. Song. http://en.wikipedia.org/wiki/There_Is_a_Balm_in_Gilead

Chapter 4

Humility: The Key to God's Heart

One day while babysitting my youth pastor's boys I decided to take them to the airport just for fun. I was taking aviation lessons at the time and had access to a small airport. It was before 9/11 so we could do that.

We had a great time. They crawled in the planes and pretended they were the pilots, but no flight ever occurred. No engine was started. They were just playing in the cockpit.

Anytime we do life without God's power flowing in and through us, we are playing at life. No wonder we get so frustrated when we don't seem to be getting anywhere. No wonder it can feel so hollow and empty, as if the engine hasn't even been started. It's like playing in a cockpit.

> "Self-absorption carries us away from feeling God's love."

God built us to need Him. He created us with a God-shaped hole at the core of our being. He not only wants to fill us up, like a gas tank, but to turn us on to a new level of life through His power inside of us.

Humility embraces the reality that God built us to need Him.

Humility is Strength not Weakness.

Let's take a look at two humble people from the Bible.

- **Jesus.** Jesus was in heaven with God. Jesus was God Himself, the third person in the Trinity. Yet He put on the skin of a man and came to live here with us. Amazing humility!
- **Moses.** Moses was the leader of a nation consisting of over a million people. The Bible describes him as "a very humble man, more humble than anyone else on the face of the earth."

Obviously, when God talks about humility, it has nothing to do with weakness; instead it has everything to do with being in a relationship of dependency on God.

One of the biggest mind-benders for me is the fact that our relationship with God the Father is exactly opposite of our relationship with our earthly father in the following way.

Relationship with Earthly Father	Relationship with Heavenly Father
We come into the world as helpless, totally dependent babies. As we grow, so grows our independence. This ability to do things for ourselves is proof of healthy development. The healthiest child develops to the point where he is able and willing to care for himself and his family independent of his parents' wealth.	We come to God as independent operators. Prior to recognizing our need for Him, we do everything for ourselves. Upon inviting Him into our lives we grow in dependence on Him. The healthiest child of God is the one who is the most dependent on His resources. Utter dependence is proof of maturity in God.

The one thing the Bible makes perfectly clear is that God absolutely hates pride and loves humility.

God finds our pride both offensive and humorous. I love the hilarious, tongue-in-cheek approach He shares in these two examples from the book of Isaiah:

> You turn things upside down, as if the potter were thought to be like the clay. Shall what is formed say to him who formed it, "He did not make me?" Can the pot say of the potter, "He knows nothing?"
>
> Does the ax raise itself above him who swings it, or the saw boast against him who uses it?

God is not impressed with our self-effort. He seeks our humility. It is impossible for us to be fully alive without God at the center of our lives.

Humility Requires Vulnerability.

Luke 18:9-14 tells the story of a proud Pharisee and a humble tax collector:

> To some who were confident of their own righteousness and looked down on everybody else, Jesus told this parable: "Two men went up to the temple to pray, one a Pharisee and the other a tax collector.
>
> "The Pharisee stood up and prayed about himself: 'God, I thank you that I am not like other men--robbers, evildoers, adulterers--or even like this tax collector. I fast twice a week and give a tenth of all I get.'"
>
> "But the tax collector stood at a distance. He would not even look up to heaven, but beat his breast and said, 'God, have mercy on me, a sinner.'"

"I tell you that this man, rather than the other, went home justified before God. For everyone who exalts himself will be humbled, and he who humbles himself will be exalted."

Do you tell God how wonderful you are and all the reasons why He should love you? Or, are you more inclined to be surprised and overwhelmed with gratitude about the fact that He already does?

> "One thing the Bible makes perfectly clear is that God absolutely hates pride and loves humility."

Pharisees were in the public eye. Everyone looked up to them and they spent a lot of energy creating an image that could be worshiped.

I am in the public eye. It isn't always easy to be vulnerable with God, because people don't appreciate it. In fact, it is often misconstrued for laziness, lack of concern or even pride.

I recently shared one of my honest prayers in a blog post. I'm going to share it here for two reasons:

- I was feeling the threat of being misunderstood when I prayed it. This feeling is normal for me.
- As I reread it later, I saw how it could be taken in two ways. This, too, is normal. Communication is tricky.

My posted prayer serves as a good example of how our communications with God can be proud, humble or a combination of both.

Here is the prayer:

> "The only reason I can get out of bed today is because I know You love turning my little piles of manure into beautiful flower gardens. I affirm my dependence on You and by faith trust You to prevent, protect from and/or use for Your glory any possible hurtful videos, photos or stories of me, Dave, Mark, Keren or Tim (even if they

simply present the facts). If what is next is about me, or our perfection, I resign. However, if this is about You, then here I am Lord, send me. Amen."

Part of this prayer is extremely self-centered: I want protection and I want it now. However, the *heart* of the prayer is a focus on God's role as my protection-provider.

If my prayer is viewed through the eyes of a Pharisee, one might deduce the following:

- The writer presumes to tell God under what circumstances she will serve.
- She is fatalistic.
- She is more interested in how things appear than in how they are.
- She'll quit unless she gets her own way.
- She blames God for any failures she encounters.

However, if the same prayer is read from the perspective of the tax collector, one may understand:

- The writer presumes that doing life without God is useless.
- She is realistic.
- She is aware of how things are and how they can be wrongly perceived.
- She'll be faithful, but knows she cannot be unless God is in control of her life.
- She takes full responsibility for her failures and embraces God's grace.

Most of our prayers are a mixed bag containing both self-centered and selfless requests. The great news is that God is looking for a humble heart. He is not impressed with perfectly polished motives or prose. He loves an honest heart.

Humility Leads to Real Life.

There are two definitions of life.

1. Physical birth, physical life on earth and physical death.
2. Spiritual birth, spiritual life on earth and spiritual life for eternity.

Adam and Eve had both types of life until they sinned, at which point they lost their spiritual life while retaining their earthly life.

> "It is impossible for us to be fully alive without God at the center of our lives."

It is quite possible to live our physical earthly lives without feeling loved by God. People do it all the time. The end is physical death and eternal separation from God.

Conversely, it is impossible to live a spiritually rewarding life on earth and enjoy heaven afterward without God. If you want maximum life for now and eternity, you must choose God now.

There are four types of love:

- Storge (motherly love)
- Eros (sexual love)
- Phileo (friendship love)
- Agape (God's love)

In the Bible, John tells us that **God is agape,** divine love. Understand this:

- It is possible to live our earthly lives without God, yet impossible to live spiritually without His presence in our lives.
- It is possible to love others with storge, eros and phileo love, but impossible to experience or extend God's apage love without a personal relationship with Him. (I John 4:8, 16)

Thus, as the writer of Corinthians so aptly states,

- If I speak in the tongues of men and of angels, but have not "agape," I am only a resounding gong or a clanging cymbal.
- If I have the gift of prophecy and can fathom all mysteries and all knowledge, and if I have a faith that can move mountains, but have not "agape," I am nothing.
- If I give all I possess to the poor and surrender my body to the flames, but have not "agape," I gain nothing.[1]

These are heroic things that count for "nothing" if done without God. Sure, they may serve a purpose in the here and now, but they are useless for eternity, because they are devoid of the eternally exchanged currency–God's agape love.

> "The very best we can give, if done on our own without God, is worthless."

The very best we can give, if done on our own without God, is worthless. The prophet Isaiah goes so far as to say that our best is hideous:

"All our righteous acts are like filthy rags." Isaiah 64:6

The words "filthy rags" here refer to the rags a woman used during her menstrual cycle. Disgusting. That is how God sees everything "good" we do unless we do it with Him.

Humility is About Your Power Source.

Consider the differences:

- An Olympic cyclist can pedal over 40 miles per hour (MPH)[2]
- An airplane pilot, flying the fastest plane, moves through the air at 6.7 mach, or 5,115 MPH.[3]
- An astronaut blasts into outer space at approximately 17,180 MPH.[4]

If pitted against one another in a race, their talent and training would be important, but the biggest factor would be their power source.

- You were born with a unique set of gifts and talents.
- You may or may not have invested into their development.
- Most importantly, you need to decide which power source you will use to propel you through the rest of your life, from this day forward.

Your Own Power	God's Power
A woman living the best she can, without God, can achieve great things in her allotted days on earth, but all of them will fade over time and none will provide eternal rewards.	A woman living through God's power has the ability to do things that will have an effect for eternity while bringing joy to her and everyone around her during the short span of her earthly life.

Humility is the basis for feeling loved by God. It is a requirement for eternal life and becomes the foundation upon which all earthly life is lived. Humility is the recognition that life without God is useless. It is the understanding that we can only be *truly* effective by allowing His life to flow through us.

Conversation Starters.

1. What has been your power source of choice so far in your life?
2. What are your greatest gifts and talents? How might the power and presence of God applied to them change their effectiveness?
3. Why do you think God hates pride as much as He does?
4. Do you believe that if you pray in a certain way God is obligated to answer in the way you wish? What formulas have you been using in prayer? Why?
5. If a person spends their entire life ignoring God and trying to avoid Him, do you feel God should be obligated to let that person into His heaven after they die? Why or why not?

End Notes

1. I Corinthians 13:1-3
2. http://olympics.india-server.com/olympic-records/cycling.html
3. http://www.globalaircraft.org/top50.htm
4. http://en.wikipedia.org/wiki/Space_shuttle#Launch

Chapter 5

Dealing with Feelings

Paul Lutus started sailing around the world in 1988 in a 31-foot boat. He finished his epic, solo, 30,000 mile voyage in 1991. He was mostly alone on the boat for years.

I became a mother in 1987. I became an empty nester in 2010. I've been mostly surrounded by children, guests in our home, volunteers, employees and customers.

Although our lives have been lived poles apart, our perception of *feelings* is in synch. Paul writes,

> "The power of feelings cannot be overestimated--they are the engine that drives us, the part of our lives that is hardest to share with others, and the companion of last resort. Every noble cause-- and every crazed mob--lies dormant in our feelings.[1]"

Intense situations will always trigger feelings that oppose the one feeling that matters the most; feeling loved by God. I wrote this poem to help express the diversity of painful and prideful emotions through which God's love has been made known to me throughout my life.

Feeling Loved

When the phone message said,
"Marnie, Your dad is dead,"
Disbelief and shock
Were the feelings I had.
But God was loving me.

When I realized as a child,
I was dumber than the rest,
Shame and loneliness soon
Settled into my chest.
But God was loving me.

When eleven and thin,
My mirror spoke,
"I'm fat," it said,
I bought the joke.
But God was loving me.

Facing challenges of any kind,
Worry would consume my mind,
My stomach would knot,
Until I resigned.
But God was loving me.

I found parenting hard,
And babies demanding.
Yet loved every moment,
Though fear kept expanding.
But God was loving me.

Infections, surgeries
Accidents, broken bones,
Every pain they felt,
I thought I must own.
But God was loving me.

She cannot speak well,
Her words, they all slur,
My daughter, my toddler,
Feeling terrified for her.
But God was loving me.

Then the lifeguard called,
"Rush to the beach,"
Fear and panic set in,
I began feeling grief.
But God was loving me.

That day I was spared,
What joy! Shear relief!
A feeling of safety,
Although it was brief.
But God was loving me.

Write a book? Who me?
I barely know how to read.
St. Martin's Press wants to see?
Pride stole my heart's lead.
But God was loving me.

Martha Stewart on the set,
And next, me on TV.
Our initials even matched,
Feeling proud as can be.
But God was loving me.

Tumbling down from that peak,
Ashamed, sorry and sad.
I'd acted poorly,
Embarrassing even my dad.
But God was loving me.

Though I struggled through school,
Barely making each grade,
If it had gone differently,
I'd never have met Dave.
Because God was loving me.

A car wreck, it took
For Dave's second look,
But that whole story,
Could be its own book.
Because God was loving me.

The highs and the lows,
The feelings unique.
Each serving to push
God's love out of reach.
But God was loving me.

In every moment of loneliness,
Jesus stood by my side,
Arms open and ready,
He loved me as I cried.
For God was loving me.

Simple Lessons About Feelings.

I've always loved Winnie the Pooh!
While others see me as Tigger or Roo,
It is Piglet who I can most relate to.

I love little piglet. He is so scared and timid. When he is blown away by the wind, I can feel myself being pushed around by forces bigger than life.

Piglet is always overwhelmed by everything and I can totally relate.

Most people have difficulty believing how scared and overextended I naturally feel. Because I've been willing to "do it scared," I appear to be brave and fearless. Because God has blessed me, I have been successful on many fronts. Yet, fear is by far the most common negative feeling with which I must deal.

1. Feelings are. They come plowing into my life without warning, permission or balance. They simply show up and take over my brain.
2. Feelings can be easily manipulated both from internal and external influences. They intensify based upon circumstances, my understanding of the facts or a perceived threat of any kind.

3. Feelings are important. I always want to be able to laugh and cry. If I'm afraid, I want to know it and admit it. If I feel hurt when wronged, that's wonderful, because it proves I'm alive. Feelings in themselves are not wrong. They are vital to a healthy life.
4. Feelings are often inaccurate. They are based on individual pieces of information funneled through my limited knowledge and experience. Upon collecting the rest of the facts, or viewing a situation from a different perspective, my feelings about it can change.
5. Most importantly, feelings are the number one thing "triggering" me to talk with God. Every intense emotion is an invitation for a conversation with God.

Every time I bring my emotions to God, He cares. He shares His perspective with me providing the balance I need.

Nancy Missler, author of "Way of Agape," says this about spiritual maturity and emotional self-life,

> "Whether we have been a Christian one year or 51 years, our self life will never improve with age. It's still as ugly and as self-centered now as it was the first day we believed. We cannot tame our self life.... I believe a mature Christian is one who recognizes his self life and makes the appropriate choices to give it over to God."

Emotions are usually the flag-bearers of "self life" or self-absorption. They can be volatile, intrusive, exasperating and out of control. But if we choose to view them as gifts, they can serve as a water slide straight down to a deeper, more loving relationship with God.

> "Feelings are. They come plowing into my life without warning, permission or balance. They simply show up and take over my brain."

We will always have to pay close attention to our emotions. A good goal is to get faster at identifying them and running our feelings to Jesus with the words, "God, help me understand this from Your perspective." When He does, it changes everything for the better.

Conversation Starters.

1. With which Winnie the Pooh character can you best relate and why?
2. Do your feelings usually prompt you closer or farther from God? Why do you think this is true?
3. What experience from your past has left you feeling unworthy or distant from God?
4. Have you ever seen anyone take charge of their emotions in a way that turned a negative situation into something good? What can you learn from what you observed?

End Notes.

1. *Paul Lutus.* http://www.arachnoid.com/
2. Missler, Chuck, and Nancy Missler. *The Way of Agape.* Coeur D'Alene, ID: King's High Way Ministries, 2009. Print.

Chapter 6
Hearing God

Hurriedly she zoomed down the highway toward the airport and her fast-approaching flight time, enjoying the solitude of a quiet car. In the air above, a helicopter pilot watched as two cars collided, a few miles ahead of where she was.

If only her radio had been turned on, and tuned to the right station, she would have been able to catch her flight by detouring onto one of the exit ramps between her and the blocked highway.

Hearing from God is like getting important traffic information before you get hit by life.

God flies higher than a helicopter pilot and transmits communication without limitation. Yet the steps to receiving input from Him are similar to those required to receiving simple traffic updates. Both require that we believe in their existence; that we believe they are available to us; that we know how to access their input; and that we believe their intentions toward us are good.

> "Every intense emotion is an invitation for a conversation with God."

Consider the similarities:

• The helicopter and radio station exist.	• God exists.
• The pilot is in airspace.	• God is outside of time and space.
• The pilot has a great vantage point.	• God has the best perspective possible.
• The pilot sees what's ahead before we do.	• God foresees and foreknows everything.
• The pilot is commissioned to help commuters avoid unnecessary delays.	• God is willing and ready to help us avoid unnecessary pain.
• The radio station makes it incredibly easy for us to access sky pilot warnings.	• God has made it incredibly easy for us to hear His voice.
• The station and pilot are committed to saving us time and reducing our stress.	• God loves us more than we love ourselves and is eager to help us.

Are you hearing from God on a daily basis? Are you listening for His input?

Remember, we can hear from God in a thousand ways. His voice is not limited to audible interactions. He can even speak directly to our thoughts.

Give God a Second Thought.

A feeling is a first thought. It bulldozes its way past other thoughts to the forefront of the mind. These days, as soon as I recognize any intense feeling, I choose to give God my second thought.

1. My first thought is the feeling.
2. My second thought is, "God, please help me understand this from Your perspective."

Even though I've been walking with God for many years, and I have been practicing running my emotions to Him for decades, I still often fail in one or many ways:

- I fail to identify the feeling as important.
- I fail to remember God is here.
- I fail to talk to God about it, even if I do remember Him.

My failure to stop the feeling at the first thought opens a floodgate for whatever emotions are directly behind it. At this point I fail everyone around me, because I'm now preoccupied with my own pain or pride.

But, more and more, I get to succeed.

Do you get it? God is not seeking perfect performances!

He wants our hearts. He wants us to journey from where we are to where He is taking us, one baby step at a time, holding Daddy's hand all along the way.

It's about the relationship, not the rules. It has never been about a list of things to do and God has never expected that we will succeed every time.

It's about becoming more conscious of God's presence, protection and provision in our lives. It's about our need to run every emotion to Jesus as quickly as possible to keep us at peace.

There is nothing like the emotional freedom you will find in Jesus. No amount of self-talk or counseling can give you the kind of perspective available through a personal relationship with God.

- God knows everything.
- God cares about you personally.
- God shares His information freely.
- God owns every resource.
- God is not limited by time or space.
- God created you and loves you more than any person ever could.
- God loves you so much that He sent His Son Jesus to die for you.
- God is concerned about the tiniest things in your life (like the cells supporting your body).
- God wants to help you.
- God is able, more than able, to provide the information, assistance or perspective you need in order to proceed in peace.

The Peace Barometer.

The umpire stood at home plate, watching the play unfold. It had been a big hit and there was an error in the outfield. As the runner headed around third base, she thought she could make it home. Running as fast as possible, she slid across the plate just in time for the catcher's glove to touch her hip.

> "A feeling is a first thought. It bulldozes its way past other thoughts to the forefront of the mind."

Everyone--the catcher, the batter and the entire crowd--watched to see the umpire's call. Was she safe or out?

In my mind, I feel like that runner all the time. A new emotion pops into play and I'm pretty sure I'll be okay, but not completely sure.

Can you relate?

If you look in my Bible, I have hundreds of verses underlined and highlighted. Colossians 3:15 is among them, but it is not only highlighted and underlined; it is also squared off and has an exclamation point, star, and "smiley face" next to it. It reads:

> "And let the peace from Christ rule (act as umpire continually) in your hearts [deciding and settling with finality all questions that arise in your minds].... And be thankful."

I have the word "umpire" circled. I love this word picture.

God, through His Spirit, wants to be the umpire in our minds. We no longer have to decide for ourselves whether or not we're in trouble. We can run every thought to Jesus and let God decide.

Sometimes His decisions don't match my desires. At times like this I experience a "Timmy" moment when I honestly pray, "God, I love You so much. I hate You for allowing this, but mostly I love You!"

> "There is nothing like the emotional freedom found in Jesus."

My sanity returns as I ask my selfish soul these questions: "Why do you think God owes you this? Isn't it possible He has reasons that can only be seen from His vantage point?"

When our will aligns with God's will, all conflict is gone. We are at peace with ourselves, our circumstances and with God.

Living without a spiritual umpire is like living up north without a functioning thermostat in the house. Why would you want to do that? Brrrrr!

Take Some Readings.

Just as a home thermostat turns on the furnace when the air temperature drops to a certain level, so our brain should trigger a chat with Jesus when it senses our peace beginning to fall away. It should trigger us to pray.

I call it a "Peace Barometer" because of the similarities.

Barometric Readings	Peace Readings
• Measure atmospheric pressure. • Used to forecast short term changes in weather. • Help identify surface troughs, high pressure systems and frontal boundaries.[1]	• Measure emotional stress. • Used to forecast short term changes in self-absorption. • Help identify surface wounds, deeply rooted hurts and potentially devastating mental storms.

I was once caught in a tornado. The weather forecasters knew well in advance. The police had been making rounds to be sure everyone had taken cover. But I was not "tuned in" until it was pretty late in the game. By then, all those barometric readings were useless because the tornado was upon me.

I have to say, I never want to be that close to a tornado again. As the intensity of its force hit my car, I feared for my life. It was terrifying!

Often we let emotional tornadoes sweep us away because we aren't tuned in to the warning system. Emotional wall clouds build and we never think of inviting God into our thought processes.

> "Living without a spiritual umpire is like living up north without a functioning thermostat in your house."

The great news is that Jesus loves to calm storms--even storms of our own making.

It is also true that He sometimes lets the external storms rage on, while calming the internal storm by restoring our peace. Either way, peace at the soul level is of tremendous value, both to us and to everyone around us. Watch for barometer fluctuations and run your thoughts to Jesus.

Merry-Go-Round.

My favorite analogy for run-away emotions is a fast-spinning merry-go-round that starts slow then builds momentum. Once it gets going, we cling to it for fear of being catapulted off and wounded as we land. We just hang on and enjoy the ride to the best of our ability.

Emotions can be like that.

- They start at one level and have the capacity to gain momentum.
- Every additional thought invested toward an emotion increases its intensity.

- Every thought directed toward God reduces the grip of the emotion's pull.

Remember how you stop a merry-go-round? Some brave kid sticks his tennis shoes out and puts up with the thunk-thunk-thunking until the shoes start skidding and the spinner slows to a stop.

We hang on to our negative emotions because we believe they are less painful than the alternatives. We have our reasons.

- **External pressure.** There are "pushers" in our lives. We have thoughts inside our head and people around us who tell us to stay on the ride. We hear, "Don't make waves," and "Let it run its course."
- **It's fun.** Many harmful emotions have addictive qualities. Feeling sorry for ourselves can be gratifying, in a way. Harboring vengeful thoughts can make us feel powerful.
- **We feel stuck.** Once we give our minds over to an emotion by thinking about it, thereby adding fuel to the fire, the centrifugal force makes it difficult to let go, even if we really want to release it and move on.

Emotions, like merry-go-rounds, have a purpose. Used according to their original design they are meant to draw us closer to God, like a water slide landing us smack-dab in the pool of God's grace.

Conversation Starters.

1. Do you think God owes you anything? If so, out of the whole big world of options, what exactly do you feel He owes you and why?
2. What do you do when God answers your prayers in a way you don't appreciate? Is this habit helping or hurting your relationship with Him?
3. Can you think of a time when you tuned God out on purpose or by accident? What was the result?

End Notes

1. http://en.wikipedia.org/wiki/Barometer

Chapter 7
Affirmations, Meditation & Memorization

Feeling God's Love Begins in the Mind.

As we wade through life, including the highs and lows, the disappointments and grief, our thoughts serve as faithful friends or fear-producing foes.

Proverbs 23:7 says, "For as he thinketh in his heart, so is he."

There is no way to "turn off" the stereo system inside your head. It contains *catch phrases*, messages from your past, providing a never-ending, steady-stream of input no matter what you do. This self talk plays like a broken record, helping or hurting you, building you up or tearing you down. It affects your mind, your will and your emotions.

II Corinthians 10:5 shares the only solution to negative self talk. It says, "Take every thought captive to the obedience of Christ."

The goal is to capture and oust every negative thought, replacing it with a powerful positive thought based on the truth outlined for us in Scripture.

I was fortunate enough to learn this principle as a child. During many hard experiences in my past, I consciously found nuggets of truth to program into my brain. These affirmative *catch phrases* replaced phrases of hopelessness, loneliness and despair. They now pop into my thoughts at random and opportune times. Each paves the way for my mind and heart to reconnect with God during times of trauma.

Can you imagine how wonderful it was to have "good" catch phrases playing through my mind on the day I received the news of my father's sudden death? How about the day I lay in the ambulance on the way to the hospital? What about when I got the call that Dave was on his way to the hospital with serious injuries from a snowmobiling accident?

Catch phrases help me move from mind-jam to mental freedom in a matter of moments. Difficult experiences are part of life. If you don't believe they should be, read the Bible. Practically every giant of faith experienced trauma and so will we.

Faith doesn't spare us from going through bad things. It simply ensures a positive eternal outcome and peace as we move through the process.

Catch phrases help us stop the barrage of bad thoughts in the moment so we can turn our minds back toward Jesus.

Favorite Affirmations

You already have catch phrases in your mind, good or bad, whether you know it or not. Here are some of my favorites.

> **God Can Use This for Good.** Everything that comes into my life, Satan wants to use to destroy me. Everything that comes into my life, God wants to use for my good. I choose to give everything to God for good.
>
> **There Is Time To Do Everything God Wants Me To Do.** There is not time to do everything. There is not time to do everything good.

There is not time to do everything everybody else wants me to do and there is not even time to do everything I want to do. But there *is* time to do everything God wants me to do.

Don't Lead. Follow Jesus. Anywhere with Jesus; no where without Him.

Praise Through It. I will offer up the sacrifice of praise! I choose to be as thankful today as I will be on the day I see Jesus face-to-face and understand how He protected me, sheltered me, and even blessed me through this difficult time.

All for Jesus--My Audience of One. It really doesn't matter what others think of me. It only feels like it matters. I choose to live each day for Jesus Christ. It is His, "Well done!" that I desire to hear.

Reject Fear. Seek Peace. There is NO fear in love; perfect love casts out fear. If I am fearful, I have stepped out of the conscious presence of God. At the first ripple on my calm composure, I choose to get out of the boat of fear and walk toward Jesus on the waves. I keep my eyes glued on His and He sustains me.

L.I.V.E. Live In View of Eternity. Everything I do today, in and through Christ, is storing up rewards for me in heaven. No exceptions.

Harmonize. Don't Monopolize. A tone has been set. Listen! Are you sharp or flat? Make the slight adjustment, then enjoy the process of making beautiful music with the saints.

Say Yes, Unless... When I say *yes* to one thing, I have, in actuality, said *no* to what I would have done with those resources otherwise. It is never just *yes* or *no*--it is always a combination of both. Sometimes the only way I can say *yes* to God is to say *no* to someone else.

Look Up More Than You Look Around. God is NOT fretting about this!

Reject Self-Pity. Self-pity is the mother of misery, bearing first a small pain, then eventually growing to consume all the joy I could have experienced. I reject self-pity and choose joy as quickly as possible.

Gift Jesus with Your Junk. Jesus is the only One who will ever thank me for *dumping* on Him!

Everything in the Light. I run every selfish, sinful or spiteful thought to Jesus, keeping everything in the light so Satan has nothing to use against me in the dark. This is God's will and way.

Don't Be a Jerk. I know I've been a jerk to Jesus many, many times. In the exact same way that Christ forgave me for being a jerk to Him, I choose to forgive everyone who behaves like a jerk toward me. I am able to do this through Christ, who strengthens me.

Watch for Openings. I am prepared to share my faith today. I eagerly watch for any opportunity to serve, pray, give, share or verbally communicate God's love.

Meditation Means to "Deeply Contemplate."

The act of meditation can be good or bad, depending on your focus. Some gurus have their students meditate on a particular word or sound, some prescribe a mantra and still others recommend letting the mind wander without direction.

The Psalmists advocate the practice of meditation, but unlike any of the methods I just described, we are encouraged to meditate on the person and attributes of God; to contemplate and think deeply about God's greatness.

- **Meditate** on God's unfailing love. Psalm 48:9
- **Meditate** on God's precepts and consider His ways. Psalm 119:15

- **Meditate** on God's wonders. Psalm 119:27
- **Meditate** on God's promises. Psalm 119:148
- **Meditate** on all God's works and consider what His hands have done. Ps 143:5

Scripture does not encourage meditation using mantras, an emptied mind or strange sounds. It does instruct us to meditate on God.

My favorite method of meditation is to intently focus on a passage of the Bible while memorizing it.

Now, before you rule out personal Scripture memorization as too hard or too time consuming, let me tell you a secret ... Any minutes you spend focusing on God through meditation and memorization are minutes of peace. During these times, you will feel God's love. Meditation is a direct path to a closer, more intimate relationship with Him.

How to Memorize.

Reality check: I struggle when memorizing anything!

Memorization is extremely challenging for me. In fact, true story, one of my most recent memory verses took four hours of concentrated effort to learn. I spent nearly an entire leg of a car trip working on *one* verse. Yet, I have memorized hundreds of verses. I cannot always remember them, but that's OK. It's not a competition.

The process of memorizing the verses is what provides the most value. Imagine that car trip: I spent four hours thinking about God, pondering the different angles and aspects of His characteristics and loving Him.

As we review and reflect during memorization, we meditate on the words and they begin to penetrate deeply into our minds and hearts. Then, as a bonus, we gain the residual value of having them memorized.

Because I know there are others who seriously struggle with memorization, I hired computer programmer, Douglas Brown, to code an online memorization tool for you based on my "Marnie Method of Memorization." My method originated from desperation.

I basically failed my way through school, barely graduating from the 12th grade. But one thing I did know how to do was memorize Bible verses. I had to! Every Saturday, I would stand in front of my mom's bedroom mirror fidgeting as I tried to recite my weekly quota of five verses. I couldn't go out to play until this priority was checked off the list.

> "It's a huge advantage to have a brain full of God."

During my teen years my mom coached a Bible Quiz Team and guess who got recruited? We actually won a state trophy and took third at the regional level, but far more importantly, I memorized hundreds of verses, including full chapters of the Bible.

To facilitate your understanding of the memorization tool we developed for you, it may help to know where it came from. Since my early teen years, I used a chalk board and 3x5" cards to memorize everything I needed to remember. The process went like this:

1. Write the verse on the card.
2. Flip the card over and, retaining the EXACT line breaks, write the acronym (only the 1st letter of each word).
3. On the chalk board (or white board), write the verse out again, retaining the EXACT line breaks, as on the card.
4. Read the verse out loud as it appears on the board.
5. Erase the longest word and read the entire thing again.
6. Erase the next longest word and repeat.
7. Continue until all of the words are gone and the verse can be recited from memory.

8. To reinforce the initial memorization work, I carry the card (from Step 2) with me for at least a week, reviewing the acronym side daily until ready to quote it from memory.

Doug was able to take these concepts and create a computer program that does it all. It's so cool and it's my gift to you. Request access at http://www.Marnie.com.

Using this online tool, you no longer need a white board or recipe cards.

- Open the memory tool page.
- Type (or copy and paste) the text into the memory tool.
- Copy the "results" into a Word document or Notepad.
- Print out your "cheat sheet."

Before you leave the page, allow the memorization tool to delete one word at a time, starting with the longest. Memorize it online then reinforce it by reviewing the acronyms often (using your cheat sheet).

Why Bother?

If you were never *forced* to memorize God's Word like I was, you might rationalize away the enormity of the benefits in store for you when you take time to memorize Scripture.

It's a huge advantage to have a brain full of God.

Since childhood, my mind has been consumed with eternally

"Look up more than you look around."

powerful, practical and precious thoughts. As you memorize God's words, you will enjoy them as they:

- Help you get to know God better simply by thinking about His words.
- Allow you to study the Bible anytime - even in the dark, in times of trauma and during times you don't have access to a Bible or other devotional book.
- Equip you to stand up against evil, wrong thinking or strong negative emotions.
- Provide excellent mental gymnastics to keep your mind keen.
- Serve as a filter through which you can understand God's perspective about the daily news and other life events.
- Become the basis for prayers for your family and friends.
- Help you remain at peace in the face of even the most stressful circumstances. The Word of God acts as an umpire, distinguishing between real danger and **F**alse **E**vidence **A**ppearing **R**eal.

Conversation Starters.

1. Have you ever memorized a Bible verse? Do you find that it is one of your favorites? Can you see how memorizing more might be helpful?
2. What catch phrases are you aware of in your own mind? Are they positive or negative?
3. What will it take to get you to meditate on God? Will you wait for your next trauma and then wish you had some verses memorized? Why not get going on one today? There is a list of 200 of my favorites in Appendix 3.

End Notes.

1. Douglas Brown of BrownPHP. http://www.brownphp.com

Chapter 8
Praying Scripture

Satan Fights Dirty.

When my kids were small they preyed on my weaknesses. They didn't fight fair. They had this annoying way of waiting until I couldn't defend myself to pull their shenanigans.

- I would answer the phone and they would go wacko, noisily bouncing off the walls.
- I would get sick and suddenly my obedient children would be breaking all the rules.
- I would emerge from the bathroom to find a mess in the kitchen.

Fortunately, at some point in their maturation, my children became my friends. They now want to provide *extra* support and encouragement to me when I'm most vulnerable, instead of taking advantage of me at those times.

I have a saying, "A friend supports you when you are down while an enemy strikes at your weakest point." God's enemy, Satan, is extremely cunning. He plays on our emotions. He loves to strike at our weakest point.

- He has studied human nature since the beginning of mankind.
- He can read the signs and knows when you are at your weakest.
- He is never more gratified than when he can deceive and destroy a friend of God.
- He is still feeding off his first success, when he convinced Eve to eat that apple.

Matthew 4:2 makes this huge understatement about Jesus' emotional and physical condition when Satan came upon Him in the desert: "After fasting forty days and forty nights, He was hungry."

Hunger is a gripping physical force that demands satisfaction. Your stomach growls, your brain hurts and, after forty days, you are very weak physically and emotionally. Jesus' fast included the added strain of being without human interaction for all those weeks.

> "A friend supports you when you are down. An enemy strikes at your weakest point."

So, when Satan showed up on the scene, his timing couldn't have been more promising for a kill. His approach matched the one he'd used with Eve, and the one he still uses with you and me: "For all that is in the world, the lust of the flesh, the lust of the eyes and the boastful pride of life, is not from the Father, but is from the world." (I John 2:16)

Jesus Modeled Effective Defensive Behavior.

There are three main types of temptations. They can play out in many different ways. Let's look at how Satan behaved toward Eve and

Jesus in their stories found in Genesis chapter three and Matthew chapter four.

1. The lust of the flesh says, "Do it! It will feel good!"
   a. Satan tempted Eve with a piece of luscious fruit from a forbidden tree.
   b. Satan tempted Jesus saying: "Command these stones to be made to bread."
2. The lust of the eyes says, "Go ahead! It looks like a plan!"
   a. Satan tempted Eve by pointing out how great that piece of fruit looked.
   b. Satan tempted Jesus saying: "If You are the Son of God, throw Yourself down; for it is written, 'He will give His angels charge over you, and they will bear you upon their hands, lest you strike your foot against a stone.'"
3. The boastful pride of life says, "For sure! It will increase your personal worth!"
   a. Satan sealed the deal by telling Eve, "God knows that in the day you eat of it your eyes will be opened, and you will be like God…."
   b. Satan took Jesus to a mountain peak overlooking the kingdoms of the world and tempted Him saying, "All these things I will give You, if You will prostrate Yourself before me."

Eve Gave In. Jesus Didn't.

1. Lust of the flesh.
   a. Eve started off alright, but twisted the truth a bit when she replied, "We may eat the fruit from the trees of the garden, except the fruit from the tree which is in the middle of the garden. God has said, 'You may not eat of it, neither shall you touch it, lest you die.'" [Adding requirements to God's standards makes us far more likely to fail at keeping His commands. God said not to eat the fruit, but He never said they must not even touch it.]

b. Jesus said, "It has been written, 'Man shall not live by bread alone, but by every word that comes from the mouth of God.'"
2. Lust of the eyes.
   a. Eve saw that the tree was good for food and that it was delightful to look at.
   b. Jesus said, "On the other hand, it is also written, 'You shall not tempt the Lord your God.'"
3. Boastful pride of life.
   a. Eve saw that the fruit was, "to be desired in order to make one wise."
   b. Jesus said, "Be gone, Satan! For it has been written, 'You shall worship the Lord your God, and Him alone shall you serve.'"

Eve's story ends with these words, "She took of its fruit and ate; and gave some also to her husband, and he ate. Then the eyes of them both were opened, and they knew that they were naked: and they sewed fig leaves together and made themselves coverings."

We have been covering up and hiding ourselves from God ever since.

Jesus' story ended differently. After His final victory over temptation, the next verse reads, "Then the devil departed from Him, and behold, angels came and ministered to Him."

> The choice is ours every single time.

The choice is ours every single time. When an emotion comes knocking at our mental door, we can choose to deal with it on our own, and end up ashamed, or we can run it to God through Scripture prayers, and end up being supported by all of heaven. (More about Scripture prayers in Section II.)

Talking to God in His Own Language.

The children and I were sitting around the kitchen table when I popped the trick question to my home school class of three:
"What language does God speak?" I asked.
"English, of course!" they replied.
What language do *you* think God speaks? Here are three hints:

- God spoke the Old Testament in Hebrew and the New Testament in Greek.
- According to the Vatican, "The Bible is the most widely read book in the world. It has already been translated into 2,454 different languages, but there are still 4,500 languages waiting for translation."
- The Bible tells a story we call, "The Tower of Babel," wherein it claims all the languages originated from God.

Since He created all of the languages in the world, it would seem logical that He can read, speak and write in all 6,954 languages fluently. It's we who have language barriers, not God.

God's Native Tongue.

I have come to the conclusion that God has His own heavenly language. Consider:

- clouds slamming together during a storm
- the roaring of ocean waves
- wind whistling through a cave or gently blowing through the trees
- water lapping against a beach
- the rustle of leaves blowing along the ground
- raindrops dancing in the grass

Sometimes God uses words we can understand, and when He does, His words are alive. Hebrews 4:12 tells us, "For the Word of God is living and active. Sharper than any double-edged sword, it penetrates even to dividing soul and spirit, joints and marrow; it judges the thoughts and attitudes of the heart."

God created us to need His Word. Next time a powerfully negative emotion is threatening your soul, wouldn't it be awesome to invite God to "cut away" the bad part and retain the good part? This is the power of praying God's Word.

Prayer Changes Things.

I love to pray. It accomplishes many things and God's answers to my prayers have often taken my breath away. Among the many advantages of prayer, one of my favorite things is that *prayer changes my own perspective*. As I invite God to explain things to me from His viewpoint, He does. His perspective enables me to receive His help and feel His love.

The second section of this book is full of prayers from my personal journal. Most were written during times when my circumstances resembled a storm, mostly cloudy and intimidating. Each prayer was heard by God and He answered them in His own time and way.

Even before I saw the answers, the very act of prayer served to take the focus off the traumatic thunder clouds of life and onto the reality that Jesus is here to help me--both beneath the storm, seated on the throne of my life, and above it, seated on His throne in heaven.

Flying High.

You know how, when flying in an airplane on a cloudy day, you finally burst through to sunshine? The clouds can only exist a few thousand feet up into the air. Sooner or later the plane breaks through into the realm where the sun is always shining.

Prayer serves as wings to lift us from the turmoil of life, up through the clouds, and into the very presence of the Son of God. Once we are up there in our spirits, we experience the peace and direction that we so desperately need in order to weather the storms blowing below.

I Love Dolphins.

I like to think of our situation as similar to that of dolphins:

- Dolphins are air-breathers who live in water.
- We are prayer-breathers who live on earth.

Without frequent trips to the "top" through prayer, our "air" supply soon runs low and we begin gasping … we experience shortness of breath that can lead to stress, worry, anxiety, fear and hopelessness.

As we regain our perspective through prayer, our physical and emotional equilibrium returns to a normal level where we are able to function properly, as we were designed by God.

We, like dolphins, must surface every few minutes in order to maintain a healthy perspective on life. Paul admonishes us to, "Pray without ceasing." In other words, we must never quit going up for air through prayer or we begin to suffocate.

Prayer is far more than simply requesting things of God and hoping for the best. Prayer is an interactive relationship with God Almighty.

Many of the prayers included in this book came to me following my favorite simple request:

"God, please talk to me about this from Your perspective."

In His mercy, God granted me a new view, and with it I was able to soar on wings as eagles; no longer tossed by the gale, but instead mounting the winds and riding them.

The Battle Belongs to the Lord.

Scripture clearly tells us that we are in a spiritual battle. I have this image in my mind of how prayer plays a role in that scrimmage. Though pure speculation, my concept motivates me to pray in a powerful way. It is based on Ephesians 6:17, which tells us that the sword of the Spirit is the Word of God and chapter ten of the book of Daniel, which describes a scene of prayer featuring a battle between angels and demons.

If the sword of the Spirit is the Word of God, and the heavenly angels are doing battle against the evil spirits in the unseen world, it seems to me that when we pray Scripture, it does something tangible--something that *can't* be done without our prayers.

When I pray Scripture, the picture I get in my mind is that of a *supernatural sword* being placed in the hand of an awaiting angel, equipping it to battle for God's chosen goals.

Conversation Starters.

1. What has been your toughest emotional battle to date? What made is seem harder than the others?
2. Have you ever felt hopeless? What restored your hope? If you still feel hopeless, are you beginning to believe God wants to help you?
3. How do you hear from God? Of all the ways God speaks, which is your favorite? When you have no words to speak, how do you communicate with God?
4. When was the last time you hid from God? How long did you hide and what finally brought you out?

End Notes

1. http://www.catholic.org/international/international_story.php?id=30064
2. Tower of Babel, Genesis 11
3. I Thessalonians 5:17

Chapter 9
Personalities & Prayer

It was the summer of 1997 when Dave invited me to go with him on a business trip so I could get away and relax. It was great! While he spent his days in meetings, I spent mine in our hotel room or by the pool studying books on personality types. (I can't help it! It's what I do to relax—I study something that interests me.)

Before that week-long research binge, I thought I might go crazy. Motherhood was so confusing to me. But as I studied books written by personality experts, I gained insight into the unique strengths and weaknesses of each member of my family. These new perspectives helped me connect the dots.

> **New perspectives help us connect the dots.**

I used my fresh understanding to parent with love and logic, to teach home school in a way that allowed each child to excel and to motivate our entire family to help with the projects we needed done.

Over the years I continued to study personality types and released my own personality test and type training which I encourage you to request for free at http://www.Marnie.com.

The most intriguing angle of my research was the realization that different personality types connect with God in their own unique ways. I don't know why this surprised me, but it did.

Ways I Worship.

I am an organized time manager. The food editor at the Minneapolis Star and Tribune once told me I was the most organized person she'd ever met. Yikes! It's sort of scary to be "the most" of anything. It feels extreme--like I'm out of balance, or something.

Yet, I love to maximize every minute and this super-organized side of my personality permeates everything I do, including how I relate to God.

> "My personality permeates everything I do, including how I relate to God."

This is as it should be: He created me.

In fact, God has used my determination to yield my "true" self to Him, including my super-organized "Marnie Methods," to enhance the lives of women from every continent and career path.

Even so, or possibly because of this, you might find it hard to believe that I have never been able to be consistent with a morning devotional time. Believe me, I tried! For years I would beat myself up about "missing devotions." But as I got to know God better and began to feel His love toward me in more tangible ways, I found my appetite for time alone with God increasing in tandem with my growing faith. I came to realize that He wanted *all* of me, not just a few minutes of focused attention in the morning.

Although I rarely start my day sitting in a chair with a Bible and journal on my lap, I always start my day with God. I am no longer concerned about how many minutes I do or do not spend in "devotions," because my entire life is a devotion.

I spend time with God because I enjoy Him, not so I can check it off a To Do list. I use time management techniques to grow closer to God, not to manipulate Him. I use best practices to enhance our relationship, not to minimize my time with Him.

My goal is to spend every possible moment being consciously aware of God's presence and power in my life. I no longer have the goal of impressing myself, God or anyone else with how many minutes I spent communicating with Him this morning.

You may wonder, "If you don't have a specific time for devotions, how do you stay close to God?"

It's a fair question. I am more inclined to experience God through the natural ebb and flow of life, for example,

- Before I open my eyes, I start talking with God.
- As I rise I'm sharing the Lord's prayer with Him line by line.
- As I shower and dress, I'm putting on the Spiritual armor. (See Appendix 2)
- As I use the restroom throughout the day, I spend those moments alone in a stall or bathroom to focus on Jesus.
- As I eat, I take each bite with gratitude.
- As I work, I pause frequently to look up, smile and breathe a prayer.
- As I proceed through my day, I usually have a verse in my pocket which I review often.
- As I experience any strong emotion, I run it to Jesus.
- As I greet a friend or employee, talk to someone on Skype or text one of my kids, I pray for them.
- As I see twenty minutes or two hours of potential quiet time coming my way, I plan to sneak away for a mini-retreat with God.

Praying at All Times.

Prayer is not something we ever finish. The Bible says to pray without ceasing. (I Thessalonians 5:17) Yet there are aspects of prayer we do indeed complete. For example:

- I finish praying for my food when I finish eating it. I do not continue praying for it all day long.
- When I hear a fire or ambulance siren, I pray for the victims and volunteers right then and maybe never again.
- We have a print-out of first names of the 18,000+ women I mentor over at http://www.marnie.com. I pray through several of these names every chance I get.
- I have prayed all the way through every name in our local phone book several times. When I am not sitting with the book on my lap, I'm not praying that way.

I am effectively efficient in prayer the same way I am in the rest of my life. God made me this way. I can either fight against how God created me or choose to allow Him to bring something good out of what others might deem obsessive or controlling.

> "When I worship, I do it with the same intensity and personality as I do everything else in my life."

When I worship, I do it with the same intensity and personality as I do everything else in my life. I do not cover up, dress up or try to fake my way through my relationship with God. Why should I? He is the one who created me. He made me this way for His own pleasure and unfathomable purposes.

I am encouraged in my approach as I read King David's prayers about the brevity of our time on earth and the importance of using each minute for God.

- Show me my life's end and the number of my days; let me know how fleeting is my life. (Psalm 39:4)
- Teach us to number our days aright, that we may gain a heart of wisdom. (Psalm 90:12)
- Trust in Him at all times. (Psalm 62:8)
- Praise the Lord at all times; let His praise be always on your lips. (Psalm 34:1)
- My times are in Your hands. (Psalm 31:15)

I've written dozens of songs over the years, but the first song I ever wrote was based on Psalm 31:15 and it is about time management.

> My times are in Your hands, Oh Lord,
> I trust You.
> My days, my hours, my minutes, Yours,
> They're Your due.
>
> Chorus:
> What could be so important
> That I'd wander from Your plan?
> You left mansions in heaven,
> To save me where I am.
>
> My schedule to Your loving will,
> I submit
> All the deeds I'm meant to do,
> You'll permit.
>
> My great ambitions, my hopes, my dreams,
> At Your feet.
> Only as I lay them there,
> Your will meet.

> I seem able to find the time,
> To do the things I really want to do
> But yielding all my rights is how,
> I love You!

Time is a gift. Time is a responsibility. My time belongs to God.

The Personalities in Worship.

Time management and organization are key factors for me, but you have your own style.

As you study the Bible, God will reveal His love toward you in ways that only you can understand. He is a personal God. While He wrote the Bible for everyone at once, He also included phrases throughout His book to which only you could relate. Sure, they are for everyone, but when you read one of these special lines, you perceive it from your unique history and personality, and its undercover love message will feel to you like a whispered secret between lovers, or an inside joke that no one else can appreciate. It is a part of what makes our love relationship with God so incredibly fulfilling. He is personally relating to each of us!

Do you already know your personality type? If not, take the free personality test available at http://www.Marnie.com.

> "...like a whispered secret between lovers, or an inside joke that no one else can appreciate."

The test will help you identify which of the predominant four personalities you have: Fun, Leader, Organizer or Stabilizer. Once you figure it out, read the worship expressions below.

Fun Personalities in Worship

- I love to talk, so listening during long group prayer times is tough.
- In my conversations with God, I do most of the talking.
- Journaling is not my thing. I scribble notes everywhere.
- My prayer life is like my life--constantly on, yet sporadic.
- I view God as someone with whom to have a friendship, a close personal relationship.
- I worship using my senses. I love music and movement.
- I really enjoy Christian novels, but don't ask me to read a concordance.
- When I read the Bible, I prefer a modern translation.
- I'm sort of scatterbrained, so sometimes I forget about God for awhile.
- God's grace is my favorite topic.

Leaders in Worship

- I sometimes work so hard for God that I miss out on enjoying Him.
- Scheduled prayer times are the only way to go.
- Group prayer times are great if I can be in charge.
- I often struggle with God, because He doesn't always want to line up with my agenda.
- I like knowing that God is in control all the time, so I don't have to be.
- I don't think much about grace, but I love the concept of justification.
- I worship through activism. You will find me serving God in protest marches or standing up for social responsibility.
- I worship in action. Solitude comes hard for me.
- I often feel closest to God while working on intense projects.
- I sometimes journal.
- I prefer devotional books and Bible software.

Organizers in Worship

- I feel most grateful to God when things are on time and going as planned.
- I love being near God in nature.
- The organized rhythm of music frees me to focus on God with my whole heart.
- I often feel I disappoint God.
- Just like every Bible hero, I seem to get pretty low at times. Just like they did, I hold on to my faith and find Him faithful.
- My greatest desire is to understand God more and more.
- I enjoy structure; the more, the better.
- I often feel insecure in my prayer life. I sometimes feel confident I'm doing it "the right way." I wish I could get this nailed down once and for all.
- I love to write--to journal, write letters to God, write stories and so on.
- I like deep thinkers like John Piper, Oswald Chambers and John Bunyan.
- I use a Study Bible.
- I am sometimes too busy trying to comprehend God to rest in His love for me.

Stabilizers in Worship

- Prayer is central to my peace.
- I prefer to "soak God in" through Bible reading, prayer, Scripture songs and praise music.
- Memorized prayers bring me comfort.
- I either need to teach a Bible study or be involved in a structured study like those by Beth Moore, or else I don't seem to do it.
- I like the easiest paths the best.
- I immediately loved the fact that God was Sovereign.
- Being at peace with God is my primary goal.

- I love to go to church, but it's sometimes disappointing because I prefer quieter music, communion and contemplative prayer.
- I don't journal, but I do, usually, write answers into Bible study workbooks.

It is enlightening to see how uniquely each of us approaches our Creator.

Further Study

I began offering personality training following my own intense research for the benefit of myself and immediate family. The full extent of my training materials on the topic include:

- The Personality Test (available for free from www.Marnie.com).
- The Personalities Explained (available for free from www.Marnie.com)
- The Personalities in Worship (available in the section above).

For further study, I encourage you to read or gain access to additional training from any of the excellent resources suggested in Appendix 4.

Conversation Starters.

1. What is your predominant personality type?
2. Read all four worship descriptions and highlight the ones that ring true for you.
3. What "obsession" or "weakness" of yours might God view as a strength if you let Him be your energy source?

End Notes.

1. Swedberg, Marnie. *My Time.* 1990. Song. http://www.Marnie.com/songs.php, USA.

Chapter 10
Does God Hate Prayer Lists?

I love lists and use them as if they were one of God's best ideas. I have lists everywhere. I often even pray from a list or scripted prayer. It is my nature. I utilize lists effectively in all areas of my life, even in my relationship with God.

One might argue:

- Lists are usually reserved for projects and things, so, does it offend a Holy God when we bring Him a list of prayer requests?
- Sometimes a list is a method we use to "finish" a prayer time so we can check it off a To Do list. We think, "I have completed my prayer list thus I am now done communicating with God for the day."
- Matthew 6:7 cautions: "When you pray, do not keep on babbling like pagans, for they think they will be heard because of their many words."

I propose that God loves it when I use lists to grow closer to Him based on the concept that each of us is made uniquely by God. If your personality type is organized by nature, lists dominate your horizon. It pleases God when His creation worships Him the way the blue print specified, and no two plans are exactly the same.

Luke 19:40 says that God can receive praise even from the rocks, but He prefers it from His children. "I tell you," he replied, "if they keep quiet, the stones will cry out."

One day, while singing my lungs out to God in my living room, sharing with Him one of my many unpublished songs, I had an awesome realization; there was nowhere else in the universe God could go to hear that particular song. I was it.

You are it! When you pray, you are the only person in the world who will say it in exactly the way you do. Even if you aren't a list-lover by nature, you may appreciate my perspective. Below I share two types of lists I use to support or improve my relationships with people and how each enhances my relationship with God.

Birthdays, Anniversaries & Christmas Cards.

Of all the lists I use, my contact list with special days is the most valuable because each name represents a person I know and love. Each date provides the chance to celebrate their existence or an accomplishment milestone.

Even if I don't remember to send a card or gift on time, it's still fun for me to see their names come across my calendar, because each name triggers so many thoughts. In that moment I

- remember them and the special times we've shared,
- pray for them,
- think of them and wonder how they are, and, of course,
- wish I'd gotten my act together enough to tell them on time.

When I review a list of God's names or a prayer list including names of the people I love, I experience a deep sense of connectivity and relationship. God's involvement deepens my emotional sensitivity and heightens my appreciation. In addition, I get a better grasp of the challenges God must face as He extends His love to all of humankind simultaneously, yet individually.

Grocery Lists.

Do you have one? I love my master-shopping list because it saves me time, money and hassle. I then reinvest my saved time into family, friends or other things that matter most in my life.

By keeping current with the grocery list on my refrigerator door, I don't run out of the ingredients I need to make any of my favorite recipes. I never need to run to the grocery store for a missing item; I have everything on hand. I love skipping that extra trip because I save:

- 15-45 minutes to drive, park, shop, wait in line, check out and drive home again.
- Money. Did you know that the average shopper spends four hours' worth of wages during every 17 minutes in the grocery store? Skip a visit. Save money.
- Hassle. It's a pain to run to the store for a missing ingredient or to spend time looking for a recipe to replace the one I wanted to make.

As it relates to your relationship with God through prayer, if you envision Him as the big grocery store owner in the sky, bringing a "shopping list" of your needs is exactly what He wants you to do. He invites you to bring Him your list of everything that is important to you.

- He knows you need things He can provide.
- He delights when you ask Him for things for others, too.
- He's aware of your free-will option to ignore Him as the ultimate Source.
- He loves it when you choose to bring your list to His door.

If your approach to God is through lists instead of free-flowing prose, God honors your heart. He sees that you are simply trying to connect with Him the best you know how and to serve Him the best you can understand. His opinion of you is based on His love for you, not on your perfect performance and not whether you prefer to connect through a list, nature, poetry or activism.

God Loves Lists.

Lists are critically important to organizational processes. They enhance our lives and God knows it. They include reminders that help us deal responsibly with the past, the present and the future.

God has His own lists. Read the book of Numbers or any of the Bible's many genealogies.

Possibly His favorite list is the one described as, "The Lamb's Book of Life" (Revelation 21:27). It is the list of names and records for every person who has ever lived their life in relationship with God.

When we share our lists with God in prayer, He gets it!

He loves each person about whom we pray and is honored that we chose to ask for His assistance in any matter, great or small.

Coming to God with a list shows that you

- Believe He exists.
- Trust Him to hear you.
- Honor Him by giving Him your business.

Hebrews 11:6 says, "But without faith it is impossible to please and be satisfactory to Him. For whoever would come near to God must [necessarily] believe that God exists and that He is the rewarder of those who earnestly and diligently seek Him [out]."

Conversation Starters.

1. What kind of lists do you use? Which is your favorite and why?
2. Do you have a prayer list? Who is on it? If not, can you think of anyone whose life might be better if you were praying for them? Do you think anyone has you on a prayer list?
3. Take a few minutes to generate a prayer list right now. Add the names and needs of your immediate and extended family, close friends, co-workers or other loved ones. Include any news or crises items plus the things that keep you awake at night or cause you stress.
4. Pray through your list as often as you like. Remember, God is real. He is listening for your prayers.

End Notes

1. Swedberg, Marnie. *Kitchen Shortcuts: Cost-Cutting Cuisine in the Minutes You Have.* Henderson, NV: Gifts of Encouragement, Inc., 2011. Print.

Section Two

Scripture Prayers

Writing Scripture Prayers

I have never served in the armed forces, but I do see myself as a soldier in a spiritual battle. I prepare myself in many ways. I...

- Suit-up in the spiritual armor every morning. (Details in Appendix 2)
- Engage in dedicated Bible studies.
- Memorize and meditate on Scripture passages.
- Share and teach what I have learned.
- Pray in the Spirit.

The prayers in this section came during prayer times when I was focusing on God and He was directing my thoughts. These prayers did not come from times of concordance-digging, nor during Bible studies, or even when I was preparing talks or devotionals; they are not a compilation of my meditations. They came as the Spirit led.

Most of the references you see on the prayer pages are a result of one of two simple things happening as I prayed:

1. A specific reference would come to mind, or
2. I would simply let my Bible fall open and put my finger down.

Either way, I made it a practice to write down the reference even *before* I read the verse. As a human, with limited perspective, I had a strong desire to "edit out" some of the verses to which I was led. Therefore, not wanting to omit something that God deemed valuable and wanted me to pray, I required this action of faith. Just because something doesn't seem to make sense at first glance, doesn't mean it's unimportant. God's ways often do not make sense at first glance.

During these hours spent with Jesus, I would follow Him wherever in His book He prompted me to go. The verses came to me, often one verse at a time, and I would flip to a Bible passage that I often had no idea would flow together with the ones before or after it.

I can hear many readers shuddering at such an approach--fearing the great damage that will be done as less experienced prayer warriors attempt to use such an unsafe method for developing Scripture prayers.

All I know is that the following prayers came about in this manner. I am only telling you the truth.

Besides, as an author myself, I have no doubt God knows His way around His Book well enough to accomplish the miracle I have described. The only real concern comes when a person tries to manipulate God through prayer--and that is simply not going to work. He is God.

For a seeking heart, one whose goal is to understand God's thoughts and to obey them, the process of being led by the Spirit to particular Scriptures can provide great comfort as well as clear direction.

It isn't magic, but it *is* awesome. This childlike method of following the Leader where ever He may go is very powerful.

Plus, how much harder is it for God to personally prompt us to look at a certain passage in this way than it is for Him to prompt us to remember certain words so we can look them up in a concordance?

Either way, God's words are gifts to us and the comprehension of a particular thought from Him is an answer to prayer.

Remember my failed attempt at a slumber party with God? He made it up 100 times over by giving me these prayers during middle-of-the-night rendezvous over the past decade. God often awakens me from sleep so I can meet with Him for an extended time of togetherness. In these quiet hours, I grab a Bible and prayer journal and "Follow the Leader."

Through the years, my prayer life has evolved:

- It used to be a wish list submitted to a Santa-type being in the sky
- Now it is truly a two-sided conversation with the King of the Universe where I sometimes speak, but more often I listen.

Since being trained in this manner, during extended prayer times, my relationship with God has become the air I breathe.

The growth of my prayer life mirrors the growth of my faith. As God has proven His ability to communicate with me on specific issues, my willingness to trust that it is Him speaking to me has also grown.

This growing relationship is my joy. It is the air of prayer I have been gasping for all my life. Even so, when the idea came to compile some of these prayers into a book, I was less than enthusiastic. For one thing, I would prefer to be perceived as sophisticated rather than simple. The fact that these prayers came about through a series of childlike games of Follow the Leader with God's Spirit is slightly embarrassing. Also, as you will probably notice, many prayers include the laying bare of my most wretched sin struggles. I was not excited about sharing those with anyone other than God.

But God…

I love that two-word phrase found in Ephesians 2:4 and 587 other places in the King James Version of the Bible.

It was by God's grace that I was led to understand He was asking me to share all of this with you… and I am not in the habit of withholding things from Him.

It made me realize, again, how often our thinking is not like His. "But God… would do it differently from Marnie."

After understanding His instructions, I prayed for a brave heart, compiled the prayers, and published this book. Now, my friend, it's in your hands.

My prayer is that God will use it to deepen your faith and love relationship with Him.

May your journey bring you closer to Him than you've ever dared to imagine possible.

Praying Scripture Prayers

Based on the model prayer of Jesus found in Matthew chapter six, there are several types or categories of prayer that God loves to receive.

Prayers of Praise. *Our Father which art in heaven, Hallowed be Thy name.*

God loves to be praised. Similar to an employer who highly values the applicant who understands his needs and has come to help, so our God loves to receive prayers that take into consideration who He is and what He desires.

The practice of praising Him, using the very words that He wrote first in His own book, has long been found to draw one quickly into His presence. God loves it when we praise Him like King David did throughout the Bible. God considers it a special joy when we praise Him in the midst of difficulties. These prayers He calls, "the sacrifice of praise."

Prayers for His Will To Be Done. *May Thy kingdom come and Thy will be done on earth as it is in heaven.*

What is God's will? We can find it spelled out specifically as we read through the Bible.

Again, we can know that our prayers will please God if we use prayers found in His own book. We cannot go wrong praying the prayers that He originally inspired.

Prayers of Petition. *Give us this day our daily bread.*

God knows we have needs. He also knows how we usually try to meet those needs through our own efforts. He likes to remind us of our dependence on Him by having us request even the most basic things from Him.

Prayers of Repentance. *Forgive us our sins as we forgive those who sin against us.*

Unlike what many experts in our society advocate, we are *not* to spend much time in soul-searching. The Bible tells us to do it only before taking the Lord's Supper. On all other occasions Scripture endorses the habit of asking *God* to search our souls and to convict us of sin. This keeps our focus on Christ and off ourselves.

However, when any sin is brought to our attention, we need to immediately and honestly ask God for forgiveness. We are also required to forgive anyone who has offended us.

Since God is willing to forgive us of the horrific sin of crucifying His Son, His requirement that we forgive others is just, and *it is a* requirement.

Prayers for Protection. *Lead us not into temptation but deliver us from the evil one.*

We are in a battle. The battle seems to be with people, but it's not. The battle is waged in the unseen world and only through prayer can we have any effect on its outcome.

There is some sort of agreement between God and Satan that was entered into at the moment when Adam ate of the forbidden fruit. Somehow, by Adam's act, Satan was given the rights to all human souls born after that time. Only as a person willfully chooses to turn from evil to God can they come under His protection.

These prayers are for those who have already chosen to receive the free gift of salvation offered to us through the death and resurrection of Jesus Christ, God's only Son.

Prayers of Submission. *For Thine is the Kingdom, the power and the glory for ever and ever. Amen.*

Prayer is not trying to manipulate God.

When we present our requests to God, it is altogether ridiculous to assume that by doing so we have locked Him into becoming our slave.

I've heard Christians say, "God *has to* answer my prayer the way I've asked, because He has promised to do so."

These people are unaware of the balance in prayer. Often the things we request are going to be gifted to us later. It reminds me of the day my very young son went whining to his father saying, "Daddy! Mommy says I can't grow hair on my chest like you!"

Of course he could grow hair on his chest! But not in the time frame he wanted--not that day.

Sometimes our prayers are exactly what God wants to gift us, but not in the way we've requested. Other times, God as Father, knows best and says "No."

This final category of prayer requires us to submit our will to His. Our example is Jesus in the Garden, before His crucifixion--praying fervently that God would free Him from the agony of the death that awaited Him, yet yielding completely to God's will for His life.

Prayers of Praise

Praising God for Direction

God, My Guide,

You are leading me on. How amazing that You busy Yourself with my every step, directing and establishing the exact direction in which I should go.

I delight to know that the determination of my ways is not in me. It is not in me, in a strong man or even in a man at his best to direct his own steps. My steps are ordered by You. You don't even expect me to understand my way; You only desire that I trust and obey.

God, my God forever, You are guiding, leading, instructing and teaching me. As I recognize and acknowledge You, You direct my paths and make them straight.

You give me the kind of faith that leans its entire personality on You in absolute trust and confidence in Your power, wisdom and goodness. You are helping me see that when I am in You, I have come into the gateway of heaven. It is You who are taking me briskly and cheerfully on my way (even if, like Jacob, it is walking 400 miles). My every season of duty is like "a few days" to me because of my love for You.

You have saved me from the fate of Leah--looking for love in all the wrong places.

You and You alone satisfy this heart You made.

I choose to hope in and cling to You. Thank You for reminding me always of my great lack. Only in You do I know fulfillment. Thank You for never giving up on me.

I rejoice that is it You who teach me to abandon my fears at the foot of Your cross and then to listen and obey no matter what You say. Amen.

Scriptures Reference:

Psalm 37:23, Jeremiah 10:23, Proverbs 20:24,
Psalms 48:14, 32:8, Proverbs 3:6, Hebrews 4:2,
Genesis 28:17, 29:1, 20, 31-35, 31:53, 32:10-11, 14-15

Praising God with the Saints

Light of Life,

I praise You that mercy, soul peace and love are being multiplied to _____ and me, Your dearly loved children, called by name, set apart and kept safe by You. We are Your "little ones," for we acknowledge and cleave to You.

Thank You for calling us to Your side and for letting us hear and obey You. It is You who are bringing us into sweet fellowship and saving us from making excuses. In our hearts You are reminding us that there is nothing of value save You alone. When You say, "Come!" we are coming with joy.

You have written on our hearts, HOLY TO THE LORD, and dedicated us for service and holy worship. We honor You as a Father and reverently fear You as Master. To You alone are due glory and praise.

I praise You that You are helping us do exactly as You instruct no matter how crazy it seems. You are so specific about Your will for us. Teach us to heed Your ways in every area throughout each moment of our lives.

You protect us and take vengeance for us. You make our enemies into heaps of ruin while sparing us from the hidden reefs of self-provision and self-protection.

Oh, what joy to place our trust in You alone. Let us never grumble at our lot in life nor seek our own desires. Instead, build us up in the most holy faith.

Make our lives rise higher and higher into the heavens as we pray in the Spirit more and more.

Teach us vigilance, patience, wisdom and courage.

You alone can keep us blameless and safe in joy and delightful ecstasy. To You alone be glory, splendor, majesty, might, dominion, power and authority now and forever. Amen.

Scriptures Reference:

from Jude 1-2, Mark 9:42, Luke 14:18 & 21,
Zechariah 14:20-21, Malachi 1:6, II Kings 9:1-4,
Deuteronomy 14:1-6, Jeremiah 51:36-37, Jude 12-25

Praising

Father,

All of heaven and earth praise Your name and we, Your children, praise Your faithfulness when we gather in Your house.

Who else would we praise? No one can compare to You. There is no one like You. You are so awesome that everyone who knows You fears You. Your strength and faithfulness are equally supreme, oh Lord, God of the hosts of heavenly beings.

When the seas rage and the waves rise, it takes nothing for You to still them. When the boastful taunt, You break them and scatter Your enemies with Your strong arm.

Heaven and earth are Yours. You founded them with a word. From the north to the south You are known for Your mighty arm and strong hand.

You require mercy and truth yet judge me with kindness. Teach me Your truth.

Let me hear the joyful sounds of freedom in the mornings. Let me walk in the light of Your face.

I rejoice all day and am exalted in Your righteousness for You are the glory of my strength. You are my defense and my King. Amen.

Scriptures Reference:

Psalm 89:5-18

Praising God for Worship

Father,

You are the lover of my soul. How I love You back.

Only in You can I be wise, pure, peaceable, gentle, obedient, merciful and good. You are increasing my faith and eliminating my doubts. It is You who help me be transparent and scrupulously honest.

Keep me running to the power of Your resurrection for the living water which quenches all spiritual thirst. Let me not despise the necessities of the fallen world but keep me seeking You and You alone.

I love Your messengers, even if the news they bring is death to my ears. You use them to conform me to Your image.

You give me boldness to speak Your words, every last one of them, as You prompt me to do so.

Thank You for teaching me and helping me to understand at the "instinct" level that I am receiving nothing that is not from You. You are increasing in me as You transform me by the renewing of my mind.

The best way for me to prove You is to believe in You. Help my unbelief. Let me worship You in spirit and in truth.

I desire to do what You created me to do and to finish that work. May it be my food, drink and sleep, my health and breath and pulse.

The fields are ready. Send Your reapers, Lord, and let me be among them. I praise You that You have sent me to gather where I have not planted and to reap where I have not sown. It is great joy to worship You as You bring many souls to Yourself. Amen.

Scriptures Reference:

James 3:17-18, John 20:3, 4:15,
Jeremiah 26:1-9, 12, Jonah 3:27-4:42

Praising

Good Shepherd,

I love You so much. You provide all I ever need. You lead and guide me to the best situations; not necessarily ritzy hotels or posh parties, but the very best places for You to minister to and through me.

When I am tired mentally, emotionally and physically, You restore my strength.

You alone keep me right with You. I only yield. You do all the work. Always have, always will.

I have nothing to fear from people, circumstances or Satan. You lead me every second and the only evil that will come to me will be at Your direction and will have an eternally valuable purpose. When my eyes are blind to Your work, I am so thankful that You comfort me. How I love You.

You not only provide every bite of food I need, but You plan my steps so even my enemies enjoy being around me. You anoint me with Your Spirit's oil to protect me from Satan's attacks. You give me so many blessings that they spill over to those around me.

Goodness and mercy walk with me along the way. I always have exactly what I need for each situation. You see to that in advance.

Oh, that everyone could know You and enjoy the luxury of being surrounded by Your mercy and goodness. Amen.

Scriptures Reference:

Psalm 23

Praising through the Book of Jude

Father,

I am Your servant, owned by You and kept for You. Thank You for Your mercy, peace and love.
You have given me such a great gift in salvation. You give me boldness to fight hard for my faith.
Hypocrites claim that Your mercy grants us the privilege to sin anytime. I am so grateful that You are keeping me awake physically, so I can pray, but also spiritually, so I can resist the temptation to sin.
Should any evil force come against me, I get to say, "The Lord speaks sharp words to you."
You are helping me beware of complainers, boasters and users--people who scoff at truth, divide people into groups and are worldly-minded.
You make me strong in the most holy (pure) faith and lead me by Your Spirit into prayer, keeping me in love with You.
Thank You for reminding me about heaven and granting me grace to deal with doubters. You keep me watching lest I fall into the same sin.
I am grateful that You have caused me to hate sin like You do.
Only You can save me and give me great joy. You always have had, still have and always will have glory, honor, power and the right to do anything You please. Amen.

Scriptures Reference:

Book of Jude

Prayers for God's Will to be done

Praying God's Will for My Attitude

Sovereign God,

I am so easily distracted by life's cares *and* pleasures. Please keep my love for You strong and hot. Save me from deserting You for something or someone else. Increase my activity, toil and endurance for You. Keep me awake to the wrong thoughts put forth as truth. Save me from getting tired or impatient.

Restore my love and devotion for You to the heights. I desire only and always to do Your will.

You know where I live--where Satan sits enthroned. Help me to continually tuck away in my heart, and obey through my will, the lessons You have taught me.

Set before me an open door--wide open which no one is able to shut. Remember that I have but little power and help me. I am keeping Your Word in front of me.

Keep me on fire for You. Remind me of my own wretched, pitiful, poor, blind and naked position. Please give me Your gold, wealth and white clothes.

Love me by convicting me, reproving me and chastening me. Teach me to repent with zeal.

Your love is so true and good. Help me embrace Your ways. Tear from me the wrong thinking that says Your ways are irksome, burdensome, oppressive and grievous.

Stay active in my heart so I may be ready at all times to be Your witness in this fallen world. Keep my conscience clear so You can glorify Your name through me.

Help me to desire no one, nothing and no goal more than You and You alone. Keep me focused and in love with You. Amen.

Scriptures Reference:

Revelation 2-3, I John 4:3,
II Peter 3:15-16, Luke 10:27

Praying God's Will for Our Faith

Father,

Increase my faith! Grant me faith to move mountains for You. Remove all doubt from my heart and replace it with unwavering faith in You. As I pray, may I confidently trust You to answer for Your glory.

Convict me if I am asking with wrong motives, evil or selfish desires that would cause me to be proud or distracted. Otherwise, give me the confidence to ask for what I need with complete assurance and boldness. Teach me to seek You with my whole heart, soul, mind and life.

I defy the lies of Satan that call You a liar. I worship You alone. Allow me to never tempt You or test Your power on frivolities, but keep me knocking when the need is real for You are my only hope. Keep me asking, never giving up until You answer me. You are such a great God.

Keep me in Your Word. Humble me. I pray, seek, crave and require Your empowering. I have set my heart to be always in Your presence. You are my soul's first necessity. Oh, save me from indifference or complacency. Keep calling me early so I may seek You diligently in the morning and throughout the days and nights.

When You put a prayer on my heart, keep me at it. You are the ultimate Father and You desire to give me good and advantageous gifts. Your standard is my faith and persistence. Save me from falling short of Your plans for me.

You find my disbelief to be warped, wayward, rebellious and thoroughly perverse. Increase my faith so that I may be pleasing to You.

I know vitality of life only in You. In Your Words I find joy and direction. Bring them to life in my heart. Give me boldness to believe it is You that leads me to ask and You who desires to answer.

Teach me to pray in Your name so You can answer me. Blessed thought that You desire my joy, gladness and delight to be full and complete in You.

I have confidence in You--assurance and the privilege of boldness to be sure that as I pray You will hear, answer and show Yourself powerful on my behalf. I leave this prayer now with settled and absolute faith in Your provision of all that I seek of You.

Grant me a heart of faith that I may not hesitate, doubt or disappoint You by believing Satan more than You. I believe! Forgive my unbelief. Amen.

Scriptures Reference:

Luke 10:22-24, I John 3:21, James 4:3, Hebrews 11:6, Deuteronomy 4:29, Luke 4:8, 12, 11:7, 10-11, Romans 10:17, II Chronicles 8:11, 11:16, 15:2, Proverbs 8:17, Matthew 7:7-11, 17:17, John 15:7, 16:24-26,
I John 5:14-15, James 1:8

Praying God's Will in the Face of a Hopeless Situation

Defender,

You are my Shield, my abundant compensation and my reward. You lead me where You want me to go and show me as much as You need me to see. In response I believe, trust, rely on and remain steadfast in You. You count this to me as righteousness. Amazing!

Even if every logical solution has gone by, I will persistently hope in faith for Your will to be done. My faith will not weaken when I see the utter impossibility of my circumstances. For You delight in showing Yourself powerful on my behalf.

You accept my belief in You as a credit toward my account. You view my reliance on You as a symbol of my conformity to Your divine will in purpose, thought and action. Oh, I believe!

Please God, call me Your friend, just like You called Abraham Your friend. Oh, to have an epitaph etched in Your writing that says, "_____ (your name) was a friend of God all the days of her life." Let it be so.

God, help me walk and live habitually before You in perfect, blameless, complete and wholehearted devotion. Help me do what You call me to do "on that very same day," even if the task is a big one.

Nothing is too hard for You. At Your appointed time and in Your prescribed way, Your work here will be done. If You deem me worthy, do not hide Your plans from me. I beg You for the opportunity to be Your close friend and servant. You know me, You decide. If You deem it best, then let me beg humbly for the souls of the lost, for the souls of those who now despise Your name.

Earnestly remember me. Imprint and fix me indelibly on Your mind. Be merciful to Your lost souls here and the souls of all You cause me to love. You are our only hope. Amen.

Scriptures Reference:

Genesis 15:1, 5, 6; Romans 4:18-19,
Galatians 3:6, James 2:23,
Genesis 17:1; 18:14, 17, 23-32 & 19:29

Praying for God's Will for My Life

Savior,

You are the only One to whom I can look for help and hope. You have shown mercy to Your children who have been faithful and good before You, and You have been gracious to me.
But I am only a child. I do not know how to start or finish. Here I am, among Your chosen ones. Give me an understanding heart to know Your thoughts about all matters.
I do not ask for long life, nor riches, nor for fame. I do ask for Your presence, direction and wisdom. Give me a pure heart that is able, willing and eager to listen to You and to obey.
Let me walk in Your ways and keep Your laws. Give me wisdom, understanding and the knowledge I need to do Your work among Your chosen ones.
You honor me exceedingly by living in me but I still want more. Open Your eyes both day and night toward me. Listen when I pray. Hear and forgive.
Be with me and do not leave me alone. Turn my heart toward You so I can walk in all Your ways and keep all Your words and laws. May this request be before You all the days of my life. Through the testimony of my life, may Your chosen ones see that You alone are God.
Make my whole heart true to You. Set me apart and put Your name on me forever. Keep Your eyes and heart on me. Help me walk before You with a true heart, doing what is right.
I desire to do all You command and to obey Your wishes.
Keep my heart always from other gods. May no other person, thing or desire rival You in my heart, mind, body or spirit. Should I ever begin to wander, be gracious to me by drawing me back to You. You alone are worthy of my praise and honor. Amen.

Scriptures Reference:

I Kings 3:6-9, 11-12, 14, 4:29,
8:27-30, 57-61, 9:3-6, 11:1 & 9

Praying God's Will for My Family

Father,

May it please You to speak good of me and my family. May our eyes be opened to You so we can hear Your words. May we see what You want us to see.

Let our home and lives be pleasing to You. Make us like valleys that spread Your love to many and like gardens with luscious fruit that satisfies--gardens that grow because of the River of Life flowing out through us.

May our words be like aloe and our strength in You like the cedar. May a steady stream of Your love flow through us and may our spiritual children be many. Grant us power and honor to be victors for You.

Bring our hearts out of bondage to sin and false gods. Be our Mighty Deliverer, crushing to death the habits of sin to which we have been held captive.

Make good come to all who pray for us and forgive and save our enemies for Your glory.

Make our hearts pure. Even if Satan offers us the most tempting sin, let us do nothing against Your Word.

Remind us that we must do nothing, good or bad, out of selfish motives. We need to listen to You and obey.

Give us hearts that burn with Your love and the boldness to do what we were created to do for You.

Draw us to Your heart. Bring us to Your throne in the morning and at night. May our sacrifice of praise be to You a sweet and pleasing smell.

Oh, be pleased with us. Be merciful and gracious to us. In Jesus' name, Amen.

Scriptures Reference:

Numbers 24-25:13, 28:1-8

Praying God's Will for the Church

Father,

You are my witness and You know how I long for and pursue unity in our body, the church, and how I pray for each member and love them as You grant opportunities.

We are Your field as well as Your workers. May the labor of our hearts and the produce of Your crop be above and beyond what I can ask or think.

Put it in every heart and then empower each of us to be strong in Your strength. Help us suit-up with Your armor and save us from the attacks of Satan and self.

I am asking You to take the dead hearts of our church and make them alive to You. I am asking You to create a desire, willingness and ability where none now exists. I know You are more than able to accomplish what You will to do.

Father, in Jesus' name, bring the hearts of Your people to a humble agreement with one another before You. Shatter the divided groups leaving no remnant.

Help us be as one in faith, and in knowing and loving You. Help us grow and stand high and complete, even as You did when You walked on earth.

As a body and individuals, may Your love flow freely through us. Give us kindness, satisfaction, humility, meekness, common (spiritual) sense, selfless motives, patience, clean minds, true hearts, endurance, hope and perseverance.

May the leadership of our body be pure before You. Let them lead in simplicity and godly sincerity, not with fleshly wisdom, but by the grace of God. Let their conversation be acceptable in the world and judged righteous in Your sight.

Humble us all to recognize and glory in the fact that our sufficiency is in You alone and in none other.

For Your honor, open our eyes and remove the blinders. Let the healing light of conviction, repentance and restoration shine bright among this people. Increase our faith.

My heart has purposed to give You all, not some, but all of me and my life. I do it wholeheartedly. Accept my humble offering and grant me grace to abound in every good work.

Help me not become weary in doing Your work. I desire no gift, only that fruit may abound for Your glory and honor.

Empower me to live a life that is pleasing to You. This is my earnest and constant prayer. Amen.

Scriptures Reference:

Philippians 1:8, I Corinthians 3:9,
Ephesians 6:10-11, Romans 4:17,
I Corinthians 1:10, Ephesians 4:13, I Corinthians 13:4-8,
II Corinthians 1:12, 3:5, 4:4, 9:7-8, Galatians 6:9, Philippians 4:17

Praying God's Will for Fellow Christians

Dear Jesus,

In Your awesome sovereignty You chose _____ and me to be Your own. We did not choose You first. You have chosen us to go and bear fruit, fruit that will remain because it is of You. I stand on the promise that whatever I ask in the Father's name, He will give me, because of Your sacrifice and intercession on my behalf.

Lord, let _____ and me stand today in full readiness wearing Your truthfulness, righteousness and peace, no matter how busy it gets. Father, may we ever keep our robes (cares) from tripping us up. Help us keep our chests protected by being right with You and our posture secure by trusting completely in Your power to save us.

May we please You by living by faith and not by sight. Let us do nothing unless we can do it by faith. Let the words of our mouths and the mediations of our hearts be pleasing to You. Tear from us any sin and hear our cries.

Search us completely. Let it be our heart's desire to be clean in Your eyes, not only in our own sight.

For whom have we in heaven but You? And there is none on this earth more important to us than You. When we grow weak in body and desperate in heart, be our strength. You are all we will ever need. Ever!

And now I ask You to save us. Oh, purge us of bitterness, wrath, anger, clamor, evil-talk, malice (evil feelings) and pride. Let us instead be kind to each other, forgiving and tender. Jesus, help us be exactly like You.

Break the strongholds that bind us and set us free to worship You wholeheartedly. Save us from the yoke of bondage. Open our eyes so we can see reality. Purify our hearts. You are merciful. Pour your Spirit on us.

Transform our minds as You renew our strength. Place in our hearts the strong desire to engraft Your Words which can save our souls from so much pain. Then, help us obey. Make us clean before You. Draw us to Your cleansing power and cleanse us from all filth of flesh and spirit. May we cease to do evil now.

Never let any of us be deceived into believing we are pure without Your cleansing touch. Let every word we speak be good--sweet to the soul and health to the bones. Let us not reject or despise Your gifts of grace. Amen

Scriptures Reference:

John 15:16, 14:13-14, Ephesians 6:15-16, Romans 14:23, Hebrews 11:6, Matthew 10:26, Psalms 32:8, 19:14, 66:18, 139:23-24, 38:18, 73:25-26, Ephesians 4:31-32, John 8:36, Galatians 5:1,Romans 12:2, James 1:21-22, Isaiah 1:16, II Corinthians 7:1, Proverbs 30:12, Matthew 12:35, Proverbs 16:24, Romans 11:29, Ephesians 4:7

Praying God's Will for My Desires

Daddy,

You have very specific ideas about who gets what. You have assigned me my portion and my cup. The boundary lines have fallen for me in pleasant places. I have a delightful inheritance.

You teach me how to properly request more from You. I ask you to:

1. Help me think carefully about what I want to ask.
2. Help me get down off my high horse.
3. Remind me to thank You for what You have already given Me.
4. Let me then ask for what I need.
5. Enable me to expect even more than that for which I ask.

After Caleb's daughter did these things, Caleb gave her the wells in the highland *and* in the valleys, more than she had asked.

Matthew tells us, "You (people) are bad yet you know how to give good things to your children. How much more will your Father in heaven give good things to those who ask Him?"

So, I am emboldened now to ask for......

Scriptures Reference:

Psalm 16:5-6, Joshua 15, Matthew 7:11

Prayers of Petition for My Children

Dear Heavenly Father,

Teach _____ (children's names). Give them peace. Prepare their hearts to minister to others as good stewards of Your manifold grace. Impart to each Your gifts and calling and prepare them to fulfill the purpose for which they were created.

Increase their learning. As their mother, help me know what to do and enable me to do it. Make my children understanding, wise and faithful stewards for You. Cause them to embrace Your knowledge and Your laws. Draw them powerfully toward You by helping them engraft Your Word, which has the power to save them from so much unnecessary pain.

Choose them, Lord, and draw them. They are without hope unless You save them. Cause them to receive, treasure and keep Your words. Save them from foolish entanglements as You draw them to Your heart. May they cry out for discernment and understanding. Place deep in their souls a yearning for You and may they seek You as silver and search for You as hidden treasure.

Save them from defiling their bodies. May they rather lay themselves on Your altar and serve You single-heartedly. Make of them a glory to You.

Let mercy and truth be their habit. May they fear You enough to die to self and live by faith.

Take away their selfish anger and replace it with godly peace and gentleness. Only You, Jesus, can satisfy their souls.

Make this home a gateway of heaven, where the impossible and the miraculous become the natural breath, a dwelling of peace and a place of pleasantness where brothers live in unity. Give us all patience as You establish us in Your ways and will. Amen.

Scriptures Reference:

Isaiah 54:13, I Peter 4:10, Romans 11:29,
 Ephesians 4:7, Proverbs 1:5, Hosea 4:6, James 1:21,
John 15:16, Proverbs 2:1-5, I Corinthians 3:17, Romans 12:1,
I Corinthians 10:31, Proverbs 3:3-4, Proverbs 14:27, Galatians 2:20,
Proverbs 22:24-25, Matthew 5:9, Psalms 133:1, Romans 15:5

Petition for the Unsaved

Father,

_____, my unsaved friends, need You. They do not love Your truth and are following false teaching and Satan's lies. They seem to even *want* to do what is wrong. Yet, I know that You love them. You showed it when You sent Your Son. The Son showed it when He came, died and rose again for them.

Jesus was given in full payment for their sins.

Do not give up on these lost souls. May they, even today, cry out to You for mercy. Open their eyes and call them to the safety of Your fold.

I am praying that someday each of these may join the heavens in declaring Your glory. The firmament shows Your handiwork. Every day it speaks Your praise and night by night it makes Your knowledge obvious. The heavens and earth give off no sound or action that does not glorify You. May it be so of _____.

You made a tabernacle for the sun in the heavens and there is nothing hid from the heat of it. Yet You allow it to circuit perfectly at 43,200 miles per hour (12 miles per second). A fraction off and we'd freeze or burn to death. You are an awesome Creator.

Your law is perfect. Convert these souls. Your testimony is sure, make them wise. Your statutes are right, make them rejoice. Your commandments are pure, enlighten their eyes.

May each desire You more than gold, yes, more than much fine gold; may they find You sweeter than honey. Warn them and allow them to keep Your truth so they can know a great reward.

It is impossible for any of us to know our own heart. Cleanse us from any secret faults. Keep us back from presumptuous sins. Let sin not have dominion over us; but let us be upright and innocent from great transgression. Let the words of our mouths and the meditations of our hearts be acceptable in Your sight, oh Lord. Be our strength and our redeemer. Amen.

Scriptures Reference:

II Thessalonians 2:9-12,
Romans 5:8, 1:28, Luke 18:13, Psalm 19

Petition for Fellow Christians

Father,

You know how much I love my Christian friends, _____.
Be with them now. Turn their hearts to You so they will walk in all Your ways and keep all Your words and laws. Answer my prayer and do what is right for _____ and me, day by day as we have needs. Let the whole earth know that You alone are God. Oh, help us walk in Your laws and keep Your words.

Set us apart by putting Your name on us forever. Let Your eyes and Your heart be on us always.

May we walk before You as David did with a true heart doing what is right. Help us do all that You require and obey Your laws. Give us a place with you in eternity.

Spare us from replacing You with other gods (interests, desires or goals). Do not turn away from us.

Father, it is easy to follow after our fleshly lusts and desires. It is easy to lose our hearts to anything but You. Keep our hearts faithful to You alone. When You speak to us, let us hear You and turn from our own ways.

Let us not deceive ourselves into thinking we are okay without You. Help us learn that Your opinion is all that matters. Keep us humbly fearing You.

May we seek Your wisdom as gold and Your understanding as silver. Turn our hearts from sin and to You alone. Amen.

Scriptures Reference:

I Kings 8:57-60, 9:3-6, 11:1-10,
Proverbs 6:2-17

Prayers of Petition

Petition for a Struggling Believer

Father,

    I pray today for _____. Though saved by grace, they are struggling right now. I claim their victory by faith and by the blood of the Lamb, for Jesus' sake.
    Bind Satan. Thwart his plans to steal the growth You desire to bring to Your children.
    I am strong in faith and You have filled me with courage to trust that You are bringing them into the inherited land. May they do according to all Your laws. Touch them now and meet their needs. Do not let them turn to the right or to the left, but prosper them in all they do.
    May Your words be ever in their thoughts. May they think about, believe in and obey You. Lead them to it so they may prosper, deal wisely and have good success.
    Give _____ the strength to stand against the wiles of Satan, the vigor to keep fighting when life-long habits attract them, and the courage to face the trials by fire so they can emerge like gold.
    Keep their hearts from fear and do not let them be overcome by terrible thoughts. Remind them that You are with them. What could be better or more beneficial? I praise You. They are in Your care. Hallelujah! Amen.

Scriptures Reference:

Joshua 1:3, 5-9

Petition for Straying Christians

Father,

Father, I have read Your Word and now meditate on Your grace. The wood has been laid on the altar and now I desire You to touch me with the heavenly spark needed to set me ablaze for You.

As the planets shine their brightest when in alignment with the sun, so align my will with Yours as I pray.

Bring _____ back into fellowship with You and with the saints. They are so vulnerable right now, miles from the closest neighbor. Tear from them the love of the world lest they themselves be devoured by it.

Few and evil are the days of this life. Each day I take up the cross You set before me. You alone can prompt me to set it down.

Even Job, in his early prosperity, suffered concerns, unrest and disquiet. Life is like that.

I praise You that life is short! We can ride through the storms to sunny days.

Oh, how I cry for _____ who are riding away from You in sin. Let them not be deceived by the eye of the storm. Draw them to Your heart before it is too late.

You tell me, "One day at a time."

Earth is a middle place, between heaven and hell, with some peaks and some valleys. May we not fall into the pleasures of sin for a season and lose the joy which can only come by walking with You through the temptations and out into the victory. These saints are Yours. Help them love and serve only You, Jesus. Only and always You! Amen.

Scriptures Reference:

Hebrews 10:23-25, II Timothy 4:10,
Genesis 47:9, Luke 9:23, John 3:26, Matthew 6:31,
Hebrews 11:25, James 1:12

Petition for My Pastors

Dear Savior,

Keep me awake! As the world around me sleeps, cover me with faith and hope. You died for me, so that dead or alive, I am with You.

You have ordained _____ to be my pastor/teachers. May every member of our body show them respect. Fill us with love for them and let us work together in peace.

As sisters and brothers in Your family, help us encourage the slothful, comfort the exhausted, help the weak, be patient with the slow and repay evil with good.

Fill us with joy and help us pray with thanksgiving at all times. Save us from blocking the Spirit's work or making light of Your words. May our work be built on the foundation of Christ so we will get a reward in heaven. Let us all continue to practice, cultivate and meditate upon the duties God has entrusted to us. Help us throw ourselves wholly into them as our ministry, so that our progress may be evident to all.

I pray that Pastors _____ will be vessels set apart and useful for honorable and noble purposes, consecrated and profitable to You, fit and ready for anything to which You call them; complete, well fitted and thoroughly equipped for every good work.

In prayer I commend them to You--to the One who is able to carry out Your purposes and do superabundantly, far over and above all that we dare to ask or think or even pray.

I thank You, God, for _____. I know You are always leading them in triumphal procession in Christ and through them spreading everywhere the fragrance of Your knowledge. Amen.

Scriptures Reference:

I Thessalonians 5,
I Corinthians 3:13-14, I Timothy 4:15,
II Timothy 2:21, Ephesians 3:20-21, II Corinthians 2:14

Petition for Young Girls

Father,

It is good to sing praises to You and give thanks to Your name. May _____ (young girl) grow like a palm tree, right and good before You. Give her a heart that desires You alone. May she run from anything that could distract her affections from You. You strongly desire her passionate love and devotion.

Father, may _____ be known for doing good things for people. Develop her so she may someday be a faithful wife to one of Your chosen vessels, and a good mother. Give her a spirit of hospitality and a servant's heart. Let her often show mercy to the suffering and kindness to all.

Fill her with Your spirit of truth. May she listen as You teach her everything she needs to know for life. May she learn to recognize Your voice and heed it always.

Free _____ from the lust of the flesh, the lust of the eyes and the boastful pride of life. Let her obey You and live by, through and because of Your Spirit's empowering. May she give herself wholly to You.

Bind Satan from her life. Give her the wisdom, desire and ability to stand firm against him and draw ever closer to You.

May she experience true love in You by Your Spirit, guarding her purity and doing only those things for which You created her, for Your glory and honor. Amen.

Scriptures Reference:

Psalm 92:1, 12, James 4:4-5,
I Timothy 5:10, John 14:16-17, 26,
John 10:14, I John 3:24, James 4:8-9,
II Corinthians 6:6c, John 6:38

Petition for Women in Ministry

Creator God,

    Build for Yourself a beautiful temple in the life of your servant, _____. Make her external beauty be exactly as You prescribe. May her eyes be beautiful windows to a soul fully yielded to You. May the characteristics of her life that are obvious to all be "three stories high" and a testimony of Your gracious love.

    May _____'s life be built on Your power, able to bear the weight of many weary ones resting themselves on her, yet never once puncturing a hole through her spirit.

    Work so gently on _____'s heart that never a sound of hammer or axe can be heard.

    Keep her doors open to only right and good teaching. May truth go in and find its way ever further into her heart.

    Crown _____'s temple with the cedar of Your glorious infilling.

    Remind _____ of Your will, "Obey My laws and keep My Word and then I will keep My promise with You, to live in You and not leave You alone."

    Spare _____'s Most Holy Place from any pollution of thought or deed. Cover her with pure gold. Encompass her heart with chains of gold, keeping her safe from every kind of evil. Cover the temple of her body, mind, soul and spirit--Your holy dwelling place, with gold. Protect her with Your cherubim. May palm trees and open flowers be the natural result of Your work in _____'s life. Amen.

Scriptures Reference:

I Kings 6

Prayers of Repentence

Prayer of Repentance

Father,

Oh, the desire You have placed in this heart of mine. I thirst for Your presence in my life, even as the deer pants for water. How I need You!

I rise early to meet You. I think of You all day long. I drift into sleep with You on my mind. Still, how I long to be with You, where You are.

I cry out to You. While others seem to doubt Your very existence, I can only think of You. I remember times of ecstatic worship and rejoice that they will come again. I praise You for always being here with me.

I am tempted to despair when I see so many living in defiance of Your ways. Forgive my lack of faith. You are all powerful. The power of the waterfalls and the surging of the seas--they are nothing compared to Your saving power.

Your mercy flows throughout the days and Your songs of salvation carry me through the nights. You give me songs and I sing them back to You.

Sometimes I ask You why. "Why do You tolerate sin? Why does life have to hurt so much? Why do You hold Jesus back from coming today?"

But then I remember and count myself a fool. Of course, You do not judge quickly because You desire that *every* soul should be saved.

Oh, spare me from ever doubting that You are in control and that Your plans are perfect. Let me always place my hope in You and praise You--You are my help and my God. Amen.

Scriptures Reference:

Psalm 42

Prayer of Repentance

Almighty God,

You have loved us in ways we cannot even understand.
You desire that we honor You as a Father and as our owner. I confess that I sometimes give You disrespect and irritated compliance instead of cheerful obedience and the honor you deserve.
I am guilty when I resent Your ways. I sin when I am only partially honest before You at the heart level. When I offer You anything less than my best, I displease You.
Be merciful to me. I have done these things--I deserve wrath.
You are looking for one--even one person who will honor Your name no matter the cost. You are so displeased with our complaining and reluctantly-given gifts. You reject them.
From sunrise to sunset, You make Your name great. You desire to receive perfume and gifts of purity. Then I come along and spoil it with my criticisms. I say how tired I am of working for You and give You half-hearted effort, all the while feeling self-righteous about it.
No wonder You do not fully bless my efforts.
Oh, great King, I am listening. I have set my heart to honor Your name. Please forgive me for my pride. Give me life and peace. Your name fills me with fear and wonder. I beg of You, Father, let only true teaching be in my mouth and no wrong be found on my lips. Oh, to walk with You each day, doing right and good according to Your standards. Save me from sin as I turn away from it. Instead of crying about it, I will cry out in praise to You. Amen.

Scriptures Reference:

Malachi 1:2-14; 2:2-14

Prayer of Repentance for a Demanding Spirit

God of All Patience & Forgiveness,

Forgive me now. I am Your younger son, the one demanding my inheritance here on earth before Your appointed time to give it to me. Oh, for the chance to gather back all that I have wasted.

Thank You for sparing me from harsh famine by letting me hear and learn from curative words. Indeed, working my way into your good graces is equivalent to feeding pigs. Funding myself is about as fulfilling as eating rotten corn cobs.

If I do not come to You often for nourishment, I will perish in some pigpen of my own making. Save me from it! How gracious You are to prompt my thoughts back toward You.

I have sinned against heaven and in Your sight. I am no longer worthy to be called Your son. Make me like one of Your hired hands.

How miraculous that You meet my baby steps in Your direction with open-armed celebration. You revel and feast and make merry because I have been dead to Your heart and now I am alive; I was lost in the cares of the world, but now I am found in Your ways.

Oh, let me never wander again from Your presence. Give me eyes to see Your loving-care for Your faithful sons. Tear from me the demanding spirit that needs parties, rewards and perks. Take my eyes off of those who seem to serve without pain and let my sights rest on You alone.

I know that I am always in Your care and that all You have is mine (in Your time and way).

Let me be found perfect in Your eyes. This could only be possible via the supernatural empowering of the Holy Spirit. I praise You!

Someday I long for You to reward me for acting shrewdly and prudently with the gifts You have given me; make me wise in Your eyes.

You have been testing me--make me faithful. Keep me faultlessly honest before You, my King. You have entrusted me mightily with the true riches of souls. You are so amazing.

I desire to live for, love and serve You and You alone. Save me from vain thoughts of helping Your cause. No! Show me Your ways and help me obey.

As Your chosen vessel, I sing You a tender love song. You, my beloved Savior, have excellent taste in properties and plans. The place You have chosen to own is on a very fruitful plot. How You have worked to create the perfect set of circumstances to oust Your enemies. You are planting seeds for hybrid blooms and for crops of great return. Save me from frustrating Your plans.

Take not away Your hedge; allow it not to be eaten or burned; do not break down these walls; but save us from the wrath of Your enemies. Do not lay us to waste.

God, cultivate and prune us so no briers or thorns can succeed. Send rain! May we be to You a delight, a garden of repose.

You call us to embrace the poor for Your sake. Oh yes, God, yes! Humble our haughty eyes. Bring low our thoughts of grandeur. You be exalted in justice and show Yourself holy in righteousness.

Save us from calling evil good and good evil. May we never be wise in our own eyes or shrewd in our own sight.

You, oh God, are high and lifted up. Holy, holy, holy are You, Lord of hosts; the whole earth is full of Your glory. Amen.

Scriptures Reference:

Luke 15:12-16:13, Isaiah 5:1-20 and 6:1-13

Prayer of Repentance

Father,

I am happy only when I have confessed my sins and am forgiven by You. Is there yet a false thought in my spirit? Purge me of it.

When I cling to my deceit, I am in tears and exhausted. I feel heavy and tired. As soon as I confess to You freely, You forgive me. Then my guilt and sadness are gone.

I desire to live a life pleasing to You and that is why I confess my wrongdoings. I do not want to run from You. You are my only hope. You are my hiding place. How I love to sing Your songs of freedom and joy.

You are so great! You show me where to go and teach me all I need to know. You give instructions as You watch my every move.

Spare me from a wayward heart. I do not want to force You into using bits and leathers to draw me to obedience. Sin only leads to sorrow.

No! I choose to trust in You and be blessed. I choose forgiveness. I am glad in You and full of joy, because I am right with You again. I sing for joy because my heart is pure before You.

Hallelujah! Amen.

Scriptures Reference:

Psalms 32

Prayer of Repentance from Pride

Father,

I am so humbled that You sometimes choose to use me to accomplish Your work. May I never accomplish anything but Your plans for me.

I see my pride. Keep me humble. Help me fully agree and understand that there will never be a worthy accomplishment for which I could take credit.

Whenever I say, "I did this! I understand that, or I helped him…" I am wrong. Can an axe say it is responsible for the work accomplished through it? Is the saw useful without the woodsman?

A stick of wood cannot lift up a man. A man lifts up the stick of wood.

Could my pots and pans make a meal without me?

Save me from pride! I can no more accomplish something without You than an axe could without a man to swing it or pan could with a cook.

Be merciful to me and use me to shine for You. Do as You planned before I was even born. Amen.

Scriptures Reference:

Isaiah 10

Prayer of Repentance after Accusation

Father,

Search me now. I have been accused of wrong-thinking or wrong-doing and I cannot see it. I feel I am right--but my entire goal is to be right with You, not with me, not even with others.

Spare me from Your indignation and fury by saving me from disobedience.
I beg of You to spare me from hypocrisy and pride.

You alone know my heart. As a judge, try me now. See if there exists in my mind, will or emotions any wicked or hurtful way. Forgive me!

Break my pride. Spirit, take me into the inner court with You. Let me understand Your glory.

You desire for me to put away my idols. Make every ounce of my will holy, separated and set apart for You.

Build me into a spiritual house to offer up sacrifices pleasing to You.

I desire to walk before You in faithfulness and truth, with a whole heart absolutely devoted to You, and to do what is right in Your sight.

Hear my prayer. See my tears. Deliver me from myself and from Satan.

You see it all--my sitting down, my coming in and even my raging at Your choices for me. Spare me from defiling my heart with vain thoughts and proud imaginations. I trust You. Amen.

Scriptures Reference:

Psalm 139:23-24, Isaiah 10:5-6,
Ezekiel 43:5, 9 and 12, I Peter 2:5,
Isaiah 38:3, 5, 37:28

Prayer of Repentance with Thanksgiving

Father,

Thank You for being the strength of my life. I wait for Your timing--keep my heart strong.

I cry to You alone. You are the One who finishes all things for me. I know that You favor those who fear You and I await Your mercy.

I confess my sin of _____.

I receive Your forgiveness as the awesome gift that it is.

Help me take captive all wrong thoughts, submitting my will to You alone. Take away pride. Purify my heart so good fruit can grow through my spiritual veins.

As I focus on You, may the weaknesses of those around me fade into insignificance. Remind me that the things that bother me now will look laughably small in light of eternity.

No one does good. You look for anyone who understands and looks for You. Let it be me!

Keep me free from sin and fill me with peace and joy. Help me! It is Your strength and powerful energy that will carry me through this day.

How You hate my sin. Yet You find joy when I walk with You.

May I never lobby, wire-pull or pressure others to get my own way. Let me pray in patience, faith and thanksgiving, casting all my cares on You. Amen.

Scriptures Reference:

Psalm 27:16, 27:14, 57:2, 147:11,
II Corinthians 10:5, I Peter 3:8-10, Jeremiah 17:10,
Matthew 6:22-24, Psalm 14:1-2, Psalm 38:6, 2:3-5,
Proverbs 11:20, I Peter 5:7

Prayer of Repentance to the Great God

Father,

My soul breaks forth into joy at the thought of You. You finish all things for me. In You alone I know peace and undisturbed rest.

Praise and honor be to Your name. You are more beautiful than any human could possibly be. Love pours from You, Powerful God. You are my safe place and my strength. You always help me in times of trouble.

You can do anything. Nothing can stop You. You are worthy of obedience, reverence and yieldedness. Every decision You make is perfect. Your arm is extended in righteous judgment and Your voice thunders words of superior quality. You are dressed in glory and power, honor and greatness.

The places where You live are beautiful. Oh, live in and beautify me. You are the Lord and King of all. You are my sun and safe-covering. You give favor and honor to whom You please.

You weigh every thought and have made all things for Your own purposes. You make every decision no matter how *independent* I think I am.

You look through me and know me. All You know is too much for me, it is too great to understand. It is because You rule that I can be full of joy.

But I see now that I have wronged You by _____. Please forgive me and restore my faith.

Your throne is built upon what is right and fair. You are the Lord Most High over all the earth and are due honor far above all other gods. Worthy!

I love to make Your name known among the nations. I sing praises to You and tell of all Your great works. My heart looks to You. You make me glad.

Help me look for Your face at all times. Give me strength to love You wholly. You are the sole desire of my heart. May my life reflect Your glory as You purify me. Amen.

Scriptures Reference:

Psalm 57:2, 4:8, 100:4, 45:2, 46;1,
Job 42:2, 40:1, 6,8-10, Psalm 84:1, 3, 10-11,
Proverbs 16:2, 33, Psalm 139:1, 6, 97:1, 2, 9, 102:27, 105:1-4

Prayers of Protection

Prayer for Protection Against Shame

Oh, Great God,

I lift to You my mind, my will and my emotions. I am vulnerable in this world, but You have power over all. I trust You.

I pray that You keep me and all Your children from shame, one of Satan's favorite spiritual tools of debilitation.

Your ways are trustworthy, but I don't understand You. Teach me! I could put my trust in money, people, talent or any number of things, but only You can save me.

You are Truth. Even if I have to wait all day, I want Your truth--not the quick-fix or drugstore version.

I know I can't grasp Your great ways. Please be patient with me and protect me as I learn to rely fully on You. I love You. Amen.

Scriptures Reference:

Psalm 25

Prayer for Protection Against Feelings of Condemnation

Jesus,

Thank You that You will never accuse me before the Father, but only intercede for me.

The accuser is the law, but God has set me free from the law of sin and death.

Satan continually brings charges and accusations against me to God. How marvelous that You became the atoning sacrifice for my sins and that I am coming to know You and be more like You as You speak to the Father on my behalf. Great joy!

You've made it all so easy for me. I continue to behold You (in the Word) and You transform me into Your image from glory to glory. Hallelujah!

Thank You that I do not deliberately, knowingly or habitually practice sin. I abide in You. I do sin, but I do not want to sin. I want a heart bent on obedience, focused on You. This pleases You and is my deepest desire.

You died because You knew I could not live perfectly. You also knew Satan would constantly shame and accuse me about this.

Thank You for cautioning me about times when I feel "less than righteous." This is a deception. In Christ I am made clean.

Now that I am in You and You are in me, I cannot abide in sin without being miserable. What a gift!

You know that I will come to love You more and obey You more fully as I understand Your love for me. I lay my life down, giving it away for Your glory.

You are greater than my conscience. Your Truth sets me free from the constant burden of condemnation. Oh, praise the Lord! Amen.

Scriptures Reference:

John 5:45, I John 2:1-2,
Romans 8:1, Revelation 12:10, I John 2:2-3,
II Corinthians 3:18, I John 3:5-20

Prayer for Protection Against Faithlessness

Father,

Protect me! Sometimes I cannot even see, hear or understand You! Cleanse me of the wrong priorities that block my view and distort my perspective of You.

I know that You are accomplishing Your will through me, my body, brain, will and emotions. I am willing, Lord. Use me!

Give me childlike faith. Make my prayers splendidly audacious. You promise me that You will do for me what I cannot do for myself. Praise the Lord!

Little by little You are driving out Your enemies. I set my heart to apply itself only to You, for Your kingdom and to love You alone.

Twila Paris sings it best: "All that is Good, all that is Right ... All that is Truth, Justice, and Light; All that is Pure, Holy indeed; All that is You, is all that I need."

I refuse to panic. I will be still and know that You are God. I know that faith is a muscle which strengthens with practice. I desire to increase my strength in You in every area of my life. Give me an undivided heart.

In godly fear I reject the blare of trumpets and attention-grabbing techniques, but I delight to know You are both Publicist and Master Record Keeper.

Let me walk in Your light, nothing folded, nothing hidden. I choose to be led by Your love, not my own. Your principle is love. Your goal is my good.

Let me never act from fear. It is faith that overcomes fear.

Bless me, Father, as I do all Your work, as You direct. Call others to pray for me that my faith will not fail. My faith is weak when I demand solutions now. Remind me to wait on Your perfect timing. My investments are in Good Hands and my most noble occupation is prayer.

Satan is my defeated foe, yet I unintentionally grant him great power when I fail to believe You. Spare me! Save me from despair. Break through the clouds of doubt. Destroy despair's darkness with Your light. It is always darkest just before the dawn and challenges are always hardest just before the victory is won. It is also difficult to believe for the impossible. Yet I choose to believe. I believe in You and You alone. Amen.

Paris, Twila. *All That I Need*. 1988. Song. Star Song Music.

Scriptures Reference:

Hebrews 4:26, Isaiah 26:20, Exodus 24:30,
Psalm 46:10, Joshua 22:24, I John 5:4, Exodus 35:43

Prayer for Protection for Christians

Father,

Thank You for being the God of peace and order.

As we work for Your glory, don't let our fire for You go out for lack of wood.

Call us early and let us meditate on Your words and ways throughout the days and nights.

Give us Your wisdom. Let our faces shine for You. Make us strong, courageous and thankful.

When Your enemies become angry and enraged, ridiculing and making fun of our faith and work for You, let us cry out to You. Turn their taunts upon their own heads and let them become prey verses predator. Do not let their sins go unnoticed, for they are making it hard for Your servants and are defying Your power to stop them.

When the taunts continue, help us keep on working. If things get worse and we are tempted to fear for our safety and success, let us praise and thank You even more.

As we pray, grant us godly creativity and wisdom to continue doing Your work while keeping watch for Satan's attacks.

Grant us courageous faith as we imprint Your powerful image on our hearts. Frustrate their purpose.

Let us not resent the slower pace required due to opposition but work on, ready to rally together as needs arise.

God, fight for us!

The days are long, the work hard and the restful times brief, but we will rejoice in You. For praise is appropriate and becoming to those who are upright in heart.

We will sing a new song. Your Word is right and all Your work is done in faithfulness. Selah.

Scriptures Reference:

I Corinthians 14:33a, Proverbs 26:20,
Psalm 42:2, Ecclesiastes 8:1, Joshua 1:7,
Nehemiah 4:1, 3-9, 14-15, 17, 20-21, Psalm 33:1-4

Prayer for Protection

Father,

Help us see life from Your perspective. Help us remember the temporary nature of pain. We are only visitors in this world.

I am so lonely for You right now, for heaven and for the death of my sin nature. Save me from giving space to selfishness here on earth. Whenever I protect myself and satisfy my fleshly desires, I fight against You for my soul.

Let me live a life of obedience, one that brings silence to all who foolishly condemn Your truth before they understand You.

You have set me free, but not to do as I please. I am free to obey You. Help me do Your will at all times.

Humble me so I may show respect always. Give me Your love for all Your children. Help me fear and honor You and all authorities.

You are my Master. I cannot do all You ask except as You empower me. Save me from an independent spirit. Empower me to obey when Your requirement seems tough and cruel. If You choose to humble me when I do obey, help me praise You. In this level of obedience You take pleasure. It is part of the work You have given me to do.

You allowed Christ to suffer. I need to follow His example. You can empower me to resist the temptation to sin, lie or answer back when insulted. You can help me refrain from being vindictive or making threats.

God, teach me to leave all my cases in Your hands because You always judge fairly. Help me to gladly carry whatever load You assign me.

Do not let me wander from this type of obedience. Be my guardian. Keep me safe from all attacks.

Help me cheerfully fit into Your plans. May my life draw others to You. Give me a beautiful, quiet (unconcerned) and gentle (encouraging) heart. May I love Your ways, never snapping back or planning revenge. You alone can save me. I choose to trust in You. Amen.

Scriptures Reference:

I Peter

Prayer for Protection Against Guilt

Father,

_____, my friend, is overwhelmed with guilt right now. Show her Your truth. Bring home to her heart Your ability to forgive her completely. Who is a God like You that pardons iniquity and passes over transgression? Your compassion for us causes You to cast our sins into the deepest sea. You blot them out as a thick cloud and redeem us.

Reason with _____ now; though her sins be as scarlet, they will be white as snow. Though they be red like crimson, they will be as wool. The scarlet here refers to a double dipped and permanent stain. Oh, the matchless extent of Your love and forgiveness toward us.

Say to _____'s heart, "I, even I, am He that blots out your transgressions for My own sake and will not remember your sins."

Father, You mark it "account paid" because of Jesus' precious blood.

So serious are You about this that You have removed _____'s confessed sins as far as the east is from the west. Hallelujah!

You have taken pity on us. You remember that we are but dust.

I praise You that Your mercy is from everlasting to everlasting to those who fear You. Comfort _____'s heart now and help her accept Your absolute forgiveness. Fill her with joy. Amen.

Scriptures Reference:

Micah 7:18-19, Isaiah 1:18, 43:25,
Romans 4:8, Psalms 103:12-17

Prayer for Protection Against Cruelty

Father,

Help me listen to You and do what is right and good in Your eyes. Keep me always looking to You. You are the rock from which I was cut, the hole from which I was dug. In You alone I find comfort and true fulfillment.

You make my deserts like Eden. You make my life a garden for Your pleasure. May joy and happiness be found in me. Fill me with thanksgiving and songs of praise.

Help me listen to You and see the light of Your laws. Be right and good on my behalf. I await Your saving power and fear Your judgment, oh Lord.

I trust with hope. I look to the sky, though it will vanish; and to the earth, though it will wear out; and to people, though they will die. But You are my saving power forever.

Help me listen to You. Help me be right and good by keeping Your law in my heart.

Make me fearless when men speak strong words to me, even words of shame and antagonism. You are powerful to save Your children.

I trust in You. It was You who made a path through the sea for the Israelites and You are my salvation. You save me from oppression.

I will sing songs of joy to You. You give me joy that lasts forever. You send joy and gladness--sadness and sorrow will be no more.

You say, "I, even I, am the Lord and beside Me there is no other." Amen.

You made me and all things. I will not be afraid. No! When one speaks evil against me, I will remember my protector, the Lord of All is His name.

Put Your words in my mouth and cover me with the shadow of Your hand. I am Yours.

I am awake. Keep me awake. Awaken me early. I have tasted of Your anger and of life without Your Spirit's control. I have been lost with no one to lead me, but You spoke sharp words to me when I turned from Your ways. You called me back.

Now, my Lord, fight for me. I have confessed my sins. Please take the guilt so I can walk in Your Spirit always. Amen.

Scriptures Reference:

Isaiah 51

Prayer for Protection

Father,

I lift my soul to You. Who else can I trust? No one! I completely trust You. As I live in Your strength, do not let Your name be put to shame because of me. No, put Your enemy to shame. You are God.

Help me, Jesus! Show me what to do. Teach me how to think. Tell me where to step. I need Your truth and I'll wait for it until You are ready to help me. You alone are worthy of honor.

My sins are so offensive to You. How I marvel that Your mercy and grace are available to me because of Jesus' blood.

I praise You for leading this sinful soul into a right relationship with You. You alone draw me to truth. You help me do what is good and right. I humble my heart before You. Teach me more about Your love, Your truth and Your heart.

You desire that I love and fear, humbly reverence and worship You. How am I doing right now? Teach me how to love and fear You more. Then lead me into a deeper love relationship with You. Make our love rich and fulfilling; prosper my children and share with us the secrets You deem important to us as we walk by faith. Make clear Your will. Help us obey.

For my part, as You enable me, I will persist in focusing all my affections on You. There are always so many distractions. Keep me focused on You. Save me.

Be merciful to me. I am alone unless You are with me.

I cry out to You for help. The cares of the world, negative interactions, physical pain or exhaustion, emotional strain, they all press to gain advantage over my affections. See my pain, forgive me for my unbelief and my selfish sins. Restore me to Your grace.

The cares and concerns of my life are many. Set me free. Let me never put You to shame but always trust in You. I desire only to bring honor to Your name. Amen.

Scriptures Reference:

Psalm 25

Prayers of Submission

Prayer of Submission

Father,

I bow low to You and Your eternal nature. When I try to imagine how You could have always existed, and how together we will live for eternity, my finite mind nearly bursts. You know I cannot grasp it.

So, I join King David in praising You while yielding cheerfully to my inability to understand You. I readily acknowledge that it is quite possible for things to be true without me being able to understand them.

Babies stay close to their mothers and I will stay close to You. I will watch, listen and obey. I will hope and rejoice in my future, for it must surely put all earthly cares into perspective. Amen.

> **I Hope In You**
> My heart is not haughty
> Nor my eyes lofty
> I hope in You, I hope in You.
> I do not concern myself
> With matters too great for me.
> I hope in You, dear Lord.
> I calm and quiet
> My soul with the warm confidence
> That You are carrying me.
> Like a child with its mother,
> I trust in You.
> From now, til eternity.

Swedberg, Marnie. I Hope In You. 2004. Song. http://www.Marnie.com/songs.php, USA.

Scriptures Reference:

Psalm 131

Prayer of Submission

Father,

I will not be afraid, for You are my safe place. Give me an undivided heart toward You.

Woe is me, for I am undone. I am full of unclean thoughts, motives, words and deeds and I dwell among godless people. You alone can take away my sin and guilt. You are my atonement and I rejoice in my salvation.

I have heard Your voice saying, "Whom shall I send? Who shall go for us?" Then I said, "Here am I; send me!"

You call me to go and tell of You. I submit to the honor and responsibility of bearing Your name.

It is true that most will not understand and receive, but in Your time, many will look to You and be healed.

Let me learn in quietness, in entire submission. Remind me often of how easily I can be deceived. Keep me ever in faith, love and holiness with self-control.

Thank You that everything You have created is good and that nothing is to be thrown away or refused if I can receive it with thanksgiving, hallowing it and consecrating it by Your Word in prayer. Amen.

Scriptures Reference:

Genesis 15:1, Hosea 10:2,
Isaiah 6:5-11, I Timothy 2:11-15, 4:4-5

Prayer of Submission

Father,

As You fill me, I will look a lot like Jesus. Fill me now.

May Your Spirit rest on me: the Spirit of wisdom and understanding; the Spirit of wise words and strength; the Spirit of much learning and the fear of the Lord.

Make me glad in the fear of You.

Let me not judge by what my eyes see or decide by what my ears hear. Let me judge in a right and good way. Let me be fair in what I think. Wrap around me Your belt of truth, Your right, good and faithful thoughts.

As I see Your fruit in my life, may I remember to give thanks to You. Even though Your righteous wrath is fully due me, for Jesus' sake Your anger is turned away and You comfort me. You are the One who saves me.

I will trust and not be afraid. For You are my strength and song. You have become my Victory. As water brings joy to the thirsty, so I rejoice in Your saving power.

I give thanks to You and call on Your name. Let me become the full measure of what You planned before I was even born. Let me make known Your works among the people. Help me remember that Your name is honored.

I sing praises to You for all Your great works. May they be made known throughout the earth. I call out and sing for joy, for You are with me. Amen.

Scriptures Reference:

Isaiah 11

Prayer of Submission

Father,

Serve my life to others like a supper of good things ready for everyone who You allow to pass near me. Let it be a fine meal of the best foods displayed in a beautiful arrangement. By it, destroy the covering of sin which is over your chosen people.

I desire to be used by You in whatever capacity You deem best. I submit myself to Your choices for my life, no matter what they are.

I praise You and give thanks to Your name. You have been faithful to do all things that You planned long ago.

Now, God, be a strong place for those who cannot help themselves and for those in need because of much trouble. Be our safe place in the storm and our shadow in the heat of the sun.

Rest Your hand on my life and live through me for others. Crush Your enemies. Satan will try--but God, put his pride to shame, together with the sinful work of his hands. Bring down the high walls Satan has built for war. Lay them low. Throw them to the ground and make them dust.

I look to You for guidance and You answer me. You alone can quiet all my fears. You alone can make this mortal life yield eternal value. Use your servant to cause many to look to You, that their faces may be full of joy. As they cry to You in humility, hear them, God; save them out of all their troubles.

I have tasted and seen that You are good. I am happy as I trust in You. Amen.

Scriptures Reference:

Isaiah 25, Psalm 34

Prayer of Submission

Father,

Make me like Jesus when He walked the earth: God indwelling flesh. When others see me, may they only see You.

You see my ways and count my steps. Help me appreciate the limitations of my life.

Incredibly, You are always thinking about me. Your thoughts toward me number more than the sand. I cannot even fathom this.

Bring Your words to life in me. Act, operate, energize and affect me. Penetrate through my willfulness and mindlessness; make my spirit right with You. Expose, sift, analyze and judge the very thoughts and purposes of my heart.

I love it that Jesus completely understands. He sympathizes with me because He shared my weaknesses, physical ailments and my vulnerability to temptation. But He never gave in.

I want to be like Jesus!

I desire to stay near Your throne of grace, receiving mercy for every failure and grace to help me when I need it most.

Jesus, You understand. You prayed specifically for Your own needs. You cried out and wept tears. You learned obedience through Your times of prayer and yielding. God heard You because You were reverent as You put God's desires before Your own.

I want to live in submission to all You have ordained for me. Amen.

Scriptures Reference:

Job 31:4, Psalm 39:4, 139:17-18,
Hebrews 4:12, 15-16; 5:7-8

Prayer of Submission for the Church

Father,

May every member of Your bride, the church, be of one mind having compassion one for another. May we love the brethren and be courteous. Let no one return evil for evil or railing for railing, but the opposite: blessing!

May we hate evil and do good. Let us seek peace and pursue it. For Your eyes watch over the righteous and Your ears are open to their prayers, but Your face is against those who do evil.

As Your sheep, may we hear Your voice. Let us be known of You and follow You. Let us submit ourselves to You in every aspect of our lives.

Let us be willing to confess our faults one to another in order that we may be covered by the prayers of each other and be healed. Help us become effective prayers who ask fervently by faith for those things that You desire. Hear us, Father, and answer for Your glory.

Teach us to cast our cares on You. Be our Bread and Life. Sanctify us through Your truth. Your Word is truth. Make us one. Give us the Spirit of power, of love, and of a sound mind. Amen.

Scriptures Reference:

I Peter 3:8-12, John 10:21, James 5:6,
I Peter 5:7, John 6:48, 17:16-21, II Timothy 1:7

Prayer of Submission

Father,

I am leaning on You; relying on and confident in You. I am doing good in Your sight and committing my ways to You. I am rolling my cares on You every day. Please make my uprightness and right standing with You go forth as light in this dark place.

I choose to be quiet in my spirit and rest in You. I am waiting for You, patiently leaning myself on You.

I refuse to fret or be angry for I desire to be pure in Your eyes.

Direct and establish my steps. Delight Yourself in my life. When I fall, grasp my hand and support me.

Refine me like silver and burn away the dross, like gold, so when You try my heart, You will find it pleasing.

Give me a happy heart, which is like good medicine, and a cheerful mind to work Your healing in those with whom I come into contact. Amen.

Scriptures Reference:

Psalm 37:3, 5-9, 23-24,
Proverbs 17:3, 22

Prayer of Submission

Father,

Your riches are so great. The things You know and Your wisdom are so deep. No one can understand Your thoughts. No one can understand Your ways.

The Scriptures say, "Who knows the mind of the Lord? Who is able to tell Him what to do? Who has given first to God, that God should pay Him back?"

Everything comes from You. Your power keeps all things together. All things were made for You. May You be honored forever.

Please enable _____ and me to give our bodies to You as living sacrifices, holy and acceptable, which is our reasonable service. Give us the desire, ability and persistence to reject the world's standards and embrace You instead.

Change our lives!

First, let us accept a new mind and then help us know Your will. Finally, enable us to do Your will so we can be good and pleasing and perfect before You.

Father, thank You that You chose us to belong to Jesus. I rest in the confidence that You are still working on us and that You don't get tired or weak on our behalf.

Send out Your light and Your truth and lead us all into Your presence. Cause us to come to You in repentance so we can praise You forever.

My hope is in You alone and I will praise You again and again for Your ceaseless love toward all of Your children. Amen.

Scriptures Reference:

Romans 1:21-23, 12:1-6,
Romans 1:6, Philippians 1:6,
Isaiah 40:9, Psalm 43:3

www.Marnie.com

Appendices & Resources

Appendix 1
Jesus is the Bridge to God

Have you ever wished you could ask a question of a famous person? It's not simple, you know. Most famous people are hidden behind gatekeepers and aren't easily accessible to the general population. It's like standing on one side of a mile-wide chasm yelling to someone on the other side. Yell all you like, the person cannot hear you.

One of the perks of hosting "Marnie's Friends," my weekly online radio talk show, is that it provides a bridge for me. When I invite a famous person to join me on the air, the gatekeeper steps aside, the bridge opens and a conversation begins.

Conversing with God.

God is Holy. He is far too big, powerful and important for us to approach Him *as a friend*, except for one thing: He wants it that way. He created a bridge making it easy for us to talk with Him anytime, any day, from any place.

Envision yourself on the left side of the diagram on the next page. The Bible explains that sin creates the chasm in the middle that keeps us apart from God.

One of my life mentors, Rev. Paul Zoschke, explained the problem like this, "We, mankind, are on the left side and God is on the right. Imagine yourself standing on the shore of an ocean. Your goal is to throw a stone across the ocean to the other side where God exists. It's impossible! Our situation is hopeless."

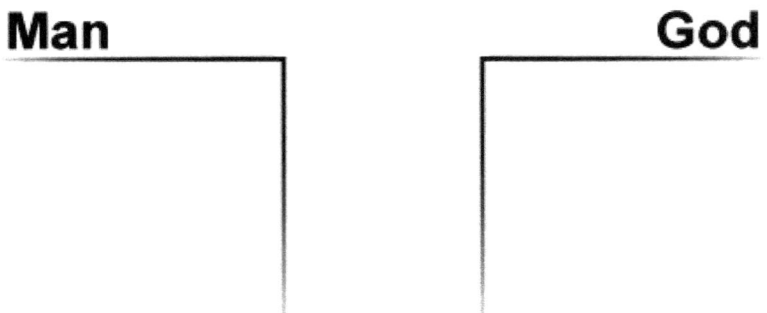

In a nutshell, this is the dilemma we face.

- God is perfect and we are not.
- No matter how hard we try (how far we throw ourselves trying to be perfect), we cannot bridge the gap.
- God is holy, perfect and righteous; we are sinful.
- Without a bridge, a way to get across the gap, we fall into the center zone trying to reach God.
- The center zone is identified in the Bible as hell.

Many people say they have lived "hell on earth." I sort of understand what they mean because life without God might be the best definition for hell.

But there is also a place called hell, the location to which spirits go after death. It is the location they chose during life (by spending their life rejecting God).

Hell is the reality of a life without God, on earth or after we die. Jesus created a bridge in the shape of a cross. He made a way for us to move from separation to connection with God.

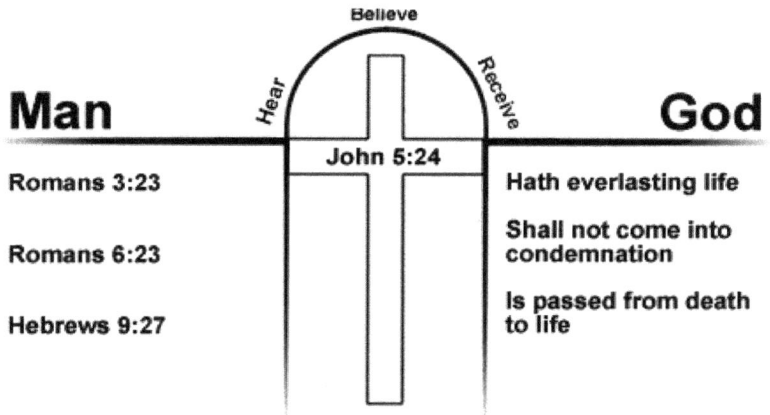

Romans 3:23 says, "For all have sinned and fall short of the glory of God." It is the picture of us falling into the center zone as we try to cross the chasm without Jesus' help.

Romans 6:23 says, "For the wages of sin is death." We deserve hell. We do not deserve to have a loving relationship with God any more than we deserve to be millionaires, just because we live in America. If we receive what our actions and attitudes deserve, we'll go to hell.

Hebrews 9:27 says, "For it is appointed for man once to die and then the judgment." Even if we pretend there is no God, and avoid thoughts of Him throughout our life on earth, we will still face Him when we die. Without the cross, without Jesus, we have made our choice: Hell.

John 5:24 says, "But to as many as hear, and believe and receive Him, to them He has given everlasting life; they shall not come into condemnation, but pass from death to life." What a fantastic verse!

If you have never crossed the bridge provided by God, why not do it right now?

- Admit that you don't deserve a relationship with God.
- Ask forgiveness for your sins.
- Trust that what Jesus did on the cross, was done for you… so you could cross the bridge of separation between you and God.
- Thank Him and live the rest of your life as if you mean it.

There is nothing that would please God more.

The Bible says that every time a person crosses that bridge, all of heaven erupts into a welcome party. Luke 15:7 says, "There will be more rejoicing in heaven over one sinner who repents than over ninety-nine righteous persons who do not need to repent."

I had my spiritual birthday party many years ago. If today is yours, send me an email at info@marnie.com. I would love to know! It is truly the most important day of your earthly life and the beginning of an amazing and endless journey.

Note: I am not sure who came up with the first rendition of the bridge illustration. I am going to attribute it to the Navigators. To learn more about the Navigators or their rendition of the bridge illustration, visit their website at http://www.navigators.org.

Appendix 2

Questions & Answers

1. Do you believe in spiritual warfare?
2. What do you do when you are attacked?
3. How do you suit-up in the spiritual armor?
4. Do you ever fast?

1. Do you believe in spiritual warfare?

I have always believed in spiritual warfare because my parents modeled balance in their approach to God and Satan. I believe that demons can actually dwell inside the minds of Christians and non-Christians alike. Satan cannot dwell in the heart or spirit of a Christian, because that is where God dwells. But I believe he can infest and retain control over portions of our mind.

I came to understand this on a personal level in 2002, when I saw a demon in my mind's eye. I actually saw him.

By the time I saw him, he was terrified, defeated and aware of the fact that he was about to be evicted from his comfy home in my mind.

Prior to that day, I didn't know I had a demon bothering me. All I knew was that I had a particular thought process that was ruining my life. No amount of fasting and prayer, Scripture memorization or meditation was helping. I was stuck!

I requested Theophostic Prayer[1]. As we met with God, He led me to a specific memory, a traumatic event in my childhood at which point I unknowingly invited a demon, disguised as the feeling of self-pity, into my life. I never knew I'd done that, but in the unseen world, I had handed the reigns of that part of my brain over to the enemy.

Exposure is the enemy's greatest weakness. As long as we believe there is no Satan, no demons and no enemy, he's got us where he wants us.

His second greatest weakness is our awareness that Satan is a defeated foe. Jesus already won the battle on the cross.

So long as we ignore, minimize or fight against evil, we will succumb to it. When we properly approach this menace, he becomes a mere irritation, like a buzzing bee with no stinger.

Addressing this topic thoroughly is not possible within this book. I encourage you to read the books in Appendix 4 and to find help from a prayer ministry whose approach to spiritual interactions agrees fully with what the Bible teaches.

2. What do you do when you are attacked?

I have adopted the "King Hezekiah" response to any and all attacks.

During the reign of King Hezekiah, there was a God-mocking nation that came to fight against Israel. They used fear tactics to dishearten the Israelites and then sent a letter of intimidation to the king. Fortunately, King Hezekiah knew what to do:

- He knelt down.
- He spread out the letter.
- He asked God to talk to Him about it from His perspective. (II Kings 19:14)

I have adopted this practice as my own. As soon as I identify a soul-threat, I kneel down, lay out the letter (or my journal entry about the verbal input) on my bed and ask God about it.

Not surprisingly, God is never worried about the things that worry me. Instead, He helps me see if there's an element of truth I must own, a sin I must confess or a wrong I must right. Then He comforts me and assures me of *His* love.

This godly input enables me to react without self-defense or retaliation. It changes everything.

Whenever the enemy flings accusations against your *big God* and His ability to save you, lay the words out before King Jesus and ask Him for wisdom, creative solutions and peace. He IS the answer to every question.

3. How do you suit-up in the spiritual armor?

It has been about a decade since I started putting on the armor every single day. I cannot believe the difference it has made in my life nor can I fathom a day without it.

- My faith has grown exponentially.
- I have been protected from direct frontal attacks physically, financially, emotionally, relationally and in every other way.
- My love and respect for God has grown immeasurably as I have seen how He entrusts me to manage a few things while He manages the universe.
- I feel God's love every morning as He provides so much spiritual protection for me personally.
- My natural state of fearfulness is much diminished as I recognize how safe I am in Christ.

The Steps I Take

You already know I do things as simply as possible, and suiting up is no exception. Thus, instead of putting each piece on in the order given in the Bible, I use the little children's song, "Head and Shoulders, Knees and Toes."

Mentally, through prayer:

1. **I pick up the shield of faith.** At first I envisioned this shield as a spiritually crafted medallion of about two and one half feet wide by four feet tall. As I continued to take it up everyday, in my spiritual mind's eye, it grew. After several months, I remember telling my Mentor-Dad, Larry Conrad, "It's so big now, I can no longer see the outside edges of it."
2. **Next I "pray on" the helmet of salvation.** This one, I believe, is to protect me from friendly fire. I have already been "saved" by Jesus Christ, so I don't need to actually get *saved* again every morning. What I do need, on a daily basis, is protection (or salvation) from my own thoughts and from the thoughts that come into my mind from friends, family and foes. I "put on the mind of Christ" and depend on Him to purify my thinking.
3. **I love strapping on the breastplate of righteousness.** My guilt regarding my unrighteousness used to debilitate me. Knowing that God sees me as perfect makes me feel safe, and safety is essential for productivity. As the Golden Gate Bridge was being built, many crew members fell to their death. Planners finally invested in a safety net, after which point productivity skyrocketed—mistakes that used to be fatal now led to a fun ride and a soft landing. Falling wasn't something workers did intentionally, as the hike back was no fun; but working hard was no longer the number one cause of death. The freedom we have to rest in God's righteousness, instead of our own, gives us the courage to work hard and fast for Jesus; because if we fall, He's there to catch us.[2]
4. **Next comes the belt of truth.** One day, while buckling on my belt, I prayed, "This is the most important one!" God said, "No. They are all important. This one feels more important to you because of your struggles to be honest." It was sometime around

this day when I understood that I was actually putting on part of God with each and every piece.

a. Belt of Truth: John 14:6
Jesus answered, "I am the way and the truth and the life. No one comes to the Father except through me."

b. Helmet of Salvation: Isaiah 12:2
"Surely God is my salvation; I will trust and not be afraid. The Lord, the Lord, is my strength and my song; He has become my salvation."

c. Breastplate of Righteousness: II Corinthians 5:21
God made Him who had no sin to be sin for us, so that in Him we might become the righteousness of God.

d. Shoes of Peace: Isaiah 9:6
For to us a child is born, to us a son is given, and the government will be on his shoulders. He will be called Wonderful Counselor, Mighty God, Everlasting Father, Prince of Peace.

5. **The last thing I put on are my shoes.** I always call them my shoes of peace, although the Bible calls them the "shoes of the preparation of the gospel of peace." I shorten it down, not out of defiance or lack of respect for the rest of the phrase, but because, for me, it is all the same: I am prepared to share my faith with anyone who asks. I look forward to it. Without God's peace, I wonder if anyone would ask.

6. **Then, I take up my sword.** This is described as "the Sword of the Spirit, which is the Word of God." Beautiful! This sword is the same one that God uses to cut through my own thoughts, to keep me in peace. It is now in my hand, to serve as a tool of healing and hope with everyone I meet. Even if I don't verbalize a verse or the name of God, the entire approach from which I address each person and situation I face each day is based on the Word of God. It's a sword that protects me always.

7. **All day long, I pray.** In the morning, the last thing I do before I finish this part of my daily routine, is thank God for the privilege of prayer. Immediately after the armor is described in Ephesians six it says, "And pray in the Spirit on all occasions with all kinds of

prayers and requests. With this in mind, be alert and always keep on praying for all the saints." Without the perpetual prayers of the day, all of this armor would be a fleeting exercise in futility.

Still, you may wonder why I want to do it every single morning. Maybe this illustration can help.

Dave and I own a black light mini golf course. When customers want to play, we turn on the lights. When they finish, we turn them off, because the bulbs are very expensive.

Every once in a while, we forget to turn the lights on and the players arrive in the area to find no lights. It takes them about one minute to let us know we've made a mistake. They *want* the black light experience.

In the same way, once we have suited up (set up the area), we must turn on the power switch as often as required. We may go minutes or hours without needing to pray about any particular emotional assault, but by suiting up each morning, we are mentally, emotionally and spiritually prepared to flip the switch of prayer at a moments notice.

By the way, I suit-up spiritually while getting dressed physically each day, as it is such an easy reminder. At first, it took me from 40 minutes to 4 hours to complete the invisible process because I was working to understand the meaning of each piece, plus I'd get distracted. Now, I can do it in as little as 30 seconds. But, honestly, most days, I don't rush. I enjoy talking to God as I take up each piece of armor He has provided for me… it's part of the love relationship we have together.

4. Do you ever fast?

In January of 2006, I wrote a typical entry in my journal which expresses my understanding of fasting and God's provision for it. I wrote:

You know what is amazing? I had wanted to fast before these women's ministry event planner teleconferences, and this A.M. You [God] had Dave challenge the Sunday School class to a 24-hour fast. For some reason I thought, "I may as well start tonight and get it over with." But tonight, just now, it occurred to me that the *desire* to fast was from You, the *assignment* to fast was from You, and now the *ability* to fast will be from You.

In all of prayer, I have come to believe that God gives us:

- the desire
- the willingness or drive
- the ability, timing or opportunities plus
- a reward for praying.

Our role in prayer reminds me of preschooler, Johnny, whose father gets up early on a Saturday morning and says, "Want to help me build a shed today?"

Little Johnny pulls on his overalls, straps on his toy tool belt and heads to the garage where he begins to "help" his dad. Pretending to saw, hammer and drill all day, Johnny does more damage than good, asks a lot of questions and slows his father down repeatedly.

Yet, at the end of the day, Johnny's dad takes him by the hand and leads him back a pace or two to survey the finished shed. Side by side, with hands on hips, they sigh with satisfaction. Then Johnny's dad looks down and says, "Wow! I could've never done it without you! Let's go get some ice cream!"

God carries us like this all the time. He lets us think we are *really* important and critical to the project, when, in fact, the only thing He really wants is our love and companionship.

The Bible tells us to fast and pray.

Next time you fast, remember, it is God who will give you the desire, God who created the sense of need for you to do it on any particular day(s), and God who will help you keep your commitment as you fast.

In the end, God will honor you for your part in the process.

End Notes.

1. Theophostic Prayer Ministry, http://www.theophostic.com
2. http://www.GoldenGateBridge.org

Appendix 3

Marnie's Top 200 Verses for Memorization & Meditation

Exodus 15:11 NIV
Who among the gods is like you, oh Lord? Who is like you—majestic in holiness, awesome in glory, working wonders?

Numbers 6:24-26 NKJV
24 The LORD bless you and keep you; 25 The LORD make His face shine upon you, and be gracious to you; 26 the LORD lift up His countenance upon you, and give you peace.

Deuteronomy 6:4-9 AMP
4 Hear, O Israel: the Lord our God is one Lord [the only Lord]. 5 And you shall love the Lord your God with all your [mind and] heart and with your entire being and with all your might. 6 And these words which I am commanding you this day shall be [first] in your [own] minds and hearts; [then] 7 You shall whet and sharpen them so as to make them penetrate, and teach and impress them diligently upon the [minds and] hearts of your children, and shall talk of them when you sit in your house and when you walk by the way, and when you lie down and when you rise up. 8 And you shall bind them as a sign upon your hand, and they shall be as frontlets (forehead bands) between your eyes. 9 And you shall write them upon the doorposts of your house and on your gates.

Deuteronomy 10:17, 20a NIV
17 For the LORD your God is God of gods and Lord of lords, the great God, mighty and awesome, who shows no partiality and accepts no bribes. 20a Fear the LORD your God and serve him.

Joshua 1:6-9 AMP
6 Be strong (confident) and of good courage, for you shall cause this people to inherit the land which I swore to their fathers to give them. 7 Only you be strong and very courageous, that you may do according to all the law which Moses My servant commanded you. Turn not from it to the right hand or to the left, that you may prosper wherever you go. 8 This Book of the Law shall not depart out of your mouth, but you shall meditate on it day and night, that you may observe and do according to all that is written in it. For then you shall make your way prosperous, and then you shall deal wisely and have good success. 9 Have not I commanded you? Be strong, vigorous, and very courageous. Be not afraid, neither be dismayed, for the Lord your God is with you wherever you go.

I Chronicles 29:11-17a, 20 NIV
11 Yours, O LORD, is the greatness and the power and the glory and the majesty and the splendor, for everything in heaven and earth is yours. Yours, O LORD, is the kingdom; you are exalted as head over all. 12 Wealth and honor come from you; you are the ruler of all things. In your hands are strength and power to exalt and give strength to all. 13 Now, our God, we give you thanks, and praise your glorious name. 14 But who am I, and who are my people, that we should be able to give as generously as this? Everything comes from you, and we have given you only what comes from your hand. 15 We are aliens and strangers in your sight, as were all our forefathers. Our days on earth are like a shadow, without hope. 16 O LORD our God, as for all this abundance that we have provided for building you a temple for your Holy Name, it comes from your hand, and all of it belongs to you. 17 I know, my God, that you test the heart and are pleased with integrity. All these things have I given willingly and with honest intent. 20 David also said to Solomon his son, Be strong and courageous, and do the work. Do not be afraid or discouraged, for the LORD God, my God, is with you. He will not fail you or forsake you until all the work for the service of the temple of the LORD is finished.

II Chronicles 7:14 NIV
If my people, who are called by my name, will humble themselves and pray and seek my face and turn from their wicked ways, then will I hear from heaven and will forgive their sin and will heal their land.

Ecclesiastes 3:11 NKJV
He has made everything beautiful in its time. Also He has put eternity in their hearts, except that no one can find out the work that God does from beginning to end.

Psalm 1:1-6, NLT
1 Oh, the joys of those who do not follow the advice of the wicked, or stand around with sinners, or join in with mockers. 2 But they delight in the law of the Lord, meditating on it day and night. 3 They are like trees planted along the riverbank, bearing fruit each season. Their leaves never wither, and they prosper in all they do. 4 But not the wicked. They are like worthless chaff, scattered by the wind. 5 They will be condemned at the time of judgment. Sinners will have no place among the godly. 6 For the Lord watches over the path of the godly, but the path of the wicked leads to destruction.

Psalm 10:4, TNIV
In their pride the wicked do not seek Him; in all their thoughts there is no room for God.

Psalm 16:5-6 NIV
5 LORD, you have assigned me my portion and my cup; you have made my lot secure. 6 The boundary lines have fallen for me in pleasant places; surely I have a delightful inheritance.

Psalm 23:1-6, KJV
The LORD is my shepherd; I shall not want. He maketh me to lie down in green pastures: he leadeth me beside the still waters. He restoreth my soul: he leadeth me in the paths of righteousness for his name's sake. Yea, though I walk through the valley of the shadow of death, I will fear no evil: for thou art with me; thy rod and thy staff they comfort me. Thou preparest a table before me in the presence of mine enemies: thou anointest my head with oil; my cup runneth over. Surely goodness and mercy shall follow me all the days of my life: and I will dwell in the house of the LORD for ever.

Psalm 31:3-5 NKJV
For You *are* my rock and my fortress; therefore, for Your name's sake, lead me and guide me. 4 Pull me out of the net which they have secretly laid for me, for You *are* my strength. 5 Into Your hand I commit my spirit; You have redeemed me, O LORD God of truth.

Psalm 91:1-16 KJV
1. He that dwelleth in the secret place of the most High shall abide under the shadow of the Almighty. 2. I will say of the LORD, He is my refuge and my fortress: my God; in him will I trust. 3. Surely he shall deliver thee from the snare of the fowler, and from the noisome pestilence. 4. He shall cover

thee with his feathers, and under his wings shalt thou trust: his truth shall be thy shield and buckler. 5. Thou shalt not be afraid for the terror by night; nor for the arrow that flieth by day; 6. Nor for the pestilence that walketh in darkness; nor for the destruction that wasteth at noonday. 7. A thousand shall fall at thy side, and ten thousand at thy right hand; but it shall not come nigh thee. 8. Only with thine eyes shalt thou behold and see the reward of the wicked. 9. Because thou hast made the LORD, which is my refuge, even the most High, thy habitation; 10. There shall no evil befall thee, neither shall any plague come nigh thy dwelling. 11. For he shall give his angels charge over thee, to keep thee in all thy ways. 12. They shall bear thee up in their hands, lest thou dash thy foot against a stone. 13. Thou shalt tread upon the lion and adder: the young lion and the dragon shalt thou trample under feet. 14. Because he hath set his love upon me, therefore will I deliver him: I will set him on high, because he hath known my name. 15. He shall call upon me, and I will answer him: I will be with him in trouble; I will deliver him, and honour him. 16. With long life will I satisfy him, and shew him my salvation.

Psalm 131:1-3 NIV
1 My heart is not proud, O LORD, my eyes are not haughty; I do not concern myself with great matters or things too wonderful for me. 2 But I have stilled and quieted my soul; like a weaned child with its mother, like a weaned child is my soul within me. 3 O, put your hope in the LORD both now and forevermore.

Proverbs 3:5-6 KJV
5 Trust in the LORD with all thine heart; and lean not unto thine own understanding. 6 In all thy ways acknowledge him, and he shall direct thy paths.

Proverbs 24:3-5, AMP
Through skillful and godly wisdom is a house (a life, a home, a family) built, and by understanding it is established [on a sound and good foundation], And by knowledge shall its chambers [of every area] be filled with all precious and pleasant riches. A wise man is strong and is better than a strong man, and a man of knowledge increases and strengthens his power;

Isaiah 32:17 NIV
The fruit of righteousness will be peace; the effect of righteousness will be quietness and confidence forever.

Isaiah 40:28-31 NKJV
28 Have you not known? Have you not heard? The everlasting God, the LORD, the Creator of the ends of the earth, neither faints nor is weary. His understanding is unsearchable. 29 He gives power to the weak, and to *those who have* no might He increases strength. 30 Even the youths shall faint and be weary, and the young men shall utterly fall, 31 But those who wait on the LORD shall renew *their* strength; they shall mount up with wings like eagles, they shall run and not be weary, they shall walk and not faint.

Isaiah 41:10 NKJV
Fear not, for I *am* with you; be not dismayed, for I *am* your God. I will strengthen you, Yes, I will help you, I will uphold you with My righteous right hand.

Isaiah 64:6 NKJV
But we are all like an unclean *thing*, and all our righteousnesses *are* like filthy rags; we all fade as a leaf, and our iniquities, like the wind, have taken us away.

Jeremiah 9:23-24, NASB
23 Thus says the LORD, "Let not a wise man boast of his wisdom, and let not the mighty man boast of his might, let not a rich man boast of his riches; 24 but let him who boasts boast of this, that he understands and knows Me, that I am the LORD who exercises lovingkindness, justice and righteousness on earth; for I delight in these things," declares the LORD.

Jeremiah 29:11 NASB
"For I know the plans that I have for you," declares the LORD, "plans for welfare and not for calamity to give you a future and a hope."

Daniel 5:23b NKJV
And you have praised the gods of silver and gold, bronze and iron, wood and stone, which do not see or hear or know; and the God who *holds* your breath in His hand and owns all your ways, you have not glorified.

Joel 2:13 NKJV
So rend your heart, and not your garments; return to the LORD your God, for He *is* gracious and merciful, slow to anger, and of great kindness; and He relents from doing harm.

Lamentations 3:22-23 KJV
22 It is of the LORD's mercies that we are not consumed, because his compassions fail not. 23 They are new every morning: great is thy faithfulness.

Jonah 2:9 NKJV
But I will sacrifice to You with the voice of thanksgiving; I will pay what I have vowed. Salvation *is* of the LORD.

Matthew 6:9-15 KJV
9 After this manner therefore pray ye: Our Father which art in heaven, Hallowed be thy name. 10 Thy kingdom come, Thy will be done in earth, as it is in heaven. 11 Give us this day our daily bread. 12 And forgive us our debts, as we forgive our debtors. 13 And lead us not into temptation, but deliver us from evil: For thine is the kingdom, and the power, and the glory, for ever. Amen. 14 For if ye forgive men their trespasses, your heavenly Father will also forgive you: 15 But if ye forgive not men their trespasses, neither will your Father forgive your trespasses.

Matthew 6:33-34 KJV
33 But seek ye first the kingdom of God, and his righteousness; and all these things shall be added unto you. 34 Take therefore no thought for the morrow: for the morrow shall take thought for the things of itself. Sufficient unto the day is the evil thereof.

Matthew 11:28 KJV
Come unto me, all ye that labour and are heavy laden, and I will give you rest.

Luke 1:45 KJV
And blessed is she that believed: for there shall be a performance of those things which were told her from the Lord.

John 1:12 NKJV
But as many as received Him, to them He gave the right to become children of God, to those who believe in His name:

John 5:30 AMP
I am able to do nothing from Myself [independently, of My own accord—but only as I am taught by God and as I get His orders]. Even as I hear, I judge [I decide as I am bidden to decide. As the voice comes to Me, so I give a decision], and My judgment is right (just, righteous), because I do not seek or consult

My own will [I have no desire to do what is pleasing to Myself, My own aim, My own purpose] but only the will and pleasure of the Father Who sent Me.

John 3:16-17 KJV
16 For God so loved the world, that he gave his only begotten Son, that whosoever believeth in him should not perish, but have everlasting life. 17For God sent not his Son into the world to condemn the world; but that the world through him might be saved.

John 6:57 AMP
Just as the living Father sent Me and I live by (through, because of) the Father, even so whoever continues to feed on Me [whoever takes Me for his food and is nourished by Me] shall [in his turn] live through and because of Me.

John 10:10b NKJV
I have come that they may have life, and that they may have *it* more abundantly.

John 10:28 NKJV
And I give them eternal life, and they shall never perish; neither shall anyone snatch them out of My hand.

John 14:6, 10, 12-13 AMP
6 Jesus said to him, I am the Way and the Truth and the Life; no one comes to the Father except by (through) Me. 10 Do you not believe that I am in the Father, and that the Father is in Me? What I am telling you I do not say on My own authority and of My own accord; but the Father Who lives continually in Me does the (His) works (His own miracles, deeds of power). 12 I assure you, most solemnly I tell you, if anyone steadfastly believes in Me, he will himself be able to do the things that I do; and he will do even greater things than these, because I go to the Father. 13 And I will do [I Myself will grant] whatever you ask in My Name [as presenting all that I AM], so that the Father may be glorified and extolled in (through) the Son.

Acts 4:12 NASB
And there is salvation in no one else; for there is no other name under heaven that has been given among men by which we must be saved.

Acts 16:31b NKJV
Believe on the Lord Jesus Christ, and you will be saved, you and your household.

Romans 4:20-22 NASB
20 yet, with respect to the promise of God, he did not waver in unbelief but grew strong in faith, giving glory to God, 21 and being fully assured that what God had promised, He was able also to perform. 22 Therefore it was also credited to him as righteousness.

Romans 5:8 NKJV
But God demonstrates His own love toward us, in that while we were still sinners, Christ died for us.

Romans 6:23 NKJV
For the wages of sin is death, but the gift of God is eternal life in Christ Jesus our Lord.

Romans 8:1 KVJ
There is therefore now no condemnation to them which are in Christ Jesus, who walk not after the flesh, but after the Spirit.

Romans 12:1-2 KJV
1 I beseech you therefore, brethren, by the mercies of God, that ye present your bodies a living sacrifice, holy, acceptable unto God, which is your reasonable service. 2 And be not conformed to this world: but be ye transformed by the renewing of your mind, that ye may prove what is that good, and acceptable, and perfect, will of God.

Romans 12:13 AMP
Contribute to the needs of God's people [sharing in the necessities of the saints]; pursue the practice of hospitality.

Romans 13:11-14 NASB
Do this, knowing the time, that it is already the hour for you to awaken from sleep; for now salvation is nearer to us than when we believed. The night is almost gone, and the day is near Therefore let us lay aside the deeds of darkness and put on the armor of light. Let us behave properly as in the day, not in carousing and drunkenness, not in sexual promiscuity and sensuality, not in strife and jealousy. But put on the Lord Jesus Christ, and make no provision for the flesh in regard to its lusts.

I Corinthians 4:2-5 NIV
2 Now it is required that those who have been given a trust must prove faithful. 3 I care very little if I am judged by you or by any human court;

indeed, I do not even judge myself. 4 My conscience is clear, but that does not make me innocent. It is the Lord who judges me. 5 Therefore judge nothing before the appointed time; wait till the Lord comes. He will bring to light what is hidden in darkness and will expose the motives of men's hearts. At that time each will receive his praise from God.

I Corinthians 6:20 NKJV

For you were bought at a price; therefore glorify God in your body and in your spirit, which are God's.

I Corinthians 9:8 NIV

And God is able to make all grace abound toward you, so that in all things, at all times, having all that you need, you may abound in every good work.

I Corinthians 10:13 NKJV

No temptation has overtaken you except such as is common to man; but God is faithful, who will not allow you to be tempted beyond what you are able, but with the temptation will also make the way of escape, that you may be able to bear *it*.

I Corinthians 13:4-8a NKJV

4 Love suffers long *and* is kind; love does not envy; love does not parade itself, is not puffed up; 5 does not behave rudely, does not seek its own, is not provoked, thinks no evil; 6 does not rejoice in iniquity, but rejoices in the truth; 7 bears all things, believes all things, hopes all things, endures all things. 8 Love never fails.

II Corinthians 3:16-18 NIV

16 But whenever anyone turns to the Lord, the veil is taken away. 17 Now the Lord is the Spirit, and where the Spirit of the Lord is, there is freedom. 18 And we, who with unveiled faces all reflect the Lord's glory, are being transformed into his likeness with ever-increasing glory, which comes from the Lord, who is the Spirit.

II Corinthians 10:3-5 NASB

3 For though we walk in the flesh, we do not war according to the flesh, 4 for the weapons of our warfare are not of the flesh, but divinely powerful for the destruction of fortresses. 5 We are destroying speculations and every lofty thing raised up against the knowledge of God, and we are taking every thought captive to the obedience of Christ,

Galatians 3:1-6 NIV

1 You foolish Galatians! Who has bewitched you? Before your very eyes Jesus Christ was clearly portrayed as crucified. 2 I would like to learn just one thing from you: Did you receive the Spirit by observing the law, or by believing what you heard? 3 Are you so foolish? After beginning with the Spirit, are you now trying to attain your goal by human effort? 4 Have you suffered so much for nothing—if it really was for nothing? 5 Does God give you his Spirit and work miracles among you because you observe the law, or because you believe what you heard? 6 Consider Abraham: "He believed God, and it was credited to him as righteousness."

Galatians 6:7-10 KJV

7 Be not deceived; God is not mocked: for whatsoever a man soweth, that shall he also reap. 8 For he that soweth to his flesh shall of the flesh reap corruption; but he that soweth to the Spirit shall of the Spirit reap life everlasting. 9 And let us not be weary in well doing: for in due season we shall reap, if we faint not. 10 As we have therefore opportunity, let us do good unto all men, especially unto them who are of the household of faith.

Ephesians 1:7 NKJV

In Him we have redemption through His blood, the forgiveness of sins, according to the riches of His grace.

Ephesians 2:4-9 AMP

4 But God—so rich is He in His mercy! Because of and in order to satisfy the great and wonderful and intense love with which He loved us, 5 Even when we were dead (slain) by [our own] shortcomings and trespasses, He made us alive together in fellowship and in union with Christ; [He gave us the very life of Christ Himself, the same new life with which He quickened Him, for] it is by grace (His favor and mercy which you did not deserve) that you are saved (delivered from judgment and made partakers of Christ's salvation). 6 And He raised us up together with Him and made us sit down together [giving us joint seating with Him] in the heavenly sphere [by virtue of our being] in Christ Jesus (the Messiah, the Anointed One). 7 He did this that He might clearly demonstrate through the ages to come the immeasurable (limitless, surpassing) riches of His free grace (His unmerited favor) in [His] kindness and goodness of heart toward us in Christ Jesus. 8 For it is by free grace (God's unmerited favor) that you are saved (delivered from judgment and made partakers of Christ's salvation) through [your] faith. This [salvation] is not of yourselves [of your own doing, it came not through your own striving], but

it is the gift of God; 9 Not because of works [not the fulfillment of the Law's demands], lest any man should boast. [It is not the result of what anyone can possibly do, so no one can pride himself in it or take glory to himself.]

Eph 6:10-18 NASB
10 Finally, be strong in the Lord and in the strength of His might. 11 Put on the full armor of God, so that you will be able to stand firm against the schemes of the devil. 12 For our struggle is not against flesh and blood, but against the rulers, against the powers, against the world forces of this darkness, against the spiritual forces of wickedness in the heavenly places. 13 Therefore, take up the full armor of God, so that you will be able to resist in the evil day, and having done everything, to stand firm. 14 Stand firm therefore, having girded your loins with truth, and having put on the breastplate of righteousness, 15 and having shod your feet with the preparation of the gospel of peace; 16 in addition to all, taking up the shield of faith with which you will be able to extinguish all the flaming arrows of the evil one. 17 And take the helmet of salvation, and the sword of the Spirit, which is the Word of God. 18 With all prayer and petition pray at all times in the Spirit, and with this in view, be on the alert with all perseverance and petition for all the saints.

Galatians 5:22-23 NASB
22 But the fruit of the Spirit is love, joy, peace, patience, kindness, goodness, faithfulness, 23 gentleness, self-control; against such things there is no law.

Philippians 1:21, KJV
For to me to live is Christ, and to die is gain.

Philippians 4:4-8 NKJV
4 Rejoice in the Lord always. Again I will say, rejoice! 5 Let your gentleness be known to all men. The Lord *is* at hand. 6 Be anxious for nothing, but in everything by prayer and supplication, with thanksgiving, let your requests be made known to God; 7 and the peace of God, which surpasses all understanding, will guard your hearts and minds through Christ Jesus. 8 Finally, brethren, whatever things are true, whatever things *are* noble, whatever things *are* just, whatever things *are* pure, whatever things *are* lovely, whatever things *are* of good report, if *there is* any virtue and if *there is* anything praiseworthy—meditate on these things.

I Thessalonians 5:16-18 KJV
16 Rejoice evermore. 17 Pray without ceasing. 18 In every thing give thanks: for this is the will of God in Christ Jesus concerning you.

II Timothy 4:18 AMP
[And indeed] the Lord will certainly deliver and draw me to Himself from every assault of evil. He will preserve and bring me safe unto His heavenly kingdom. To Him be the glory forever and ever. Amen.

Hebrews 10:5-7 AMP
Hence, when He [Christ] entered into the world, He said, Sacrifices and offerings You have not desired, but instead You have made ready a body for Me [to offer]; In burnt offerings and sin offerings You have taken no delight. Then I said, Behold, here I am, coming to do Your will, O God—[to fulfill] what is written of Me in the volume of the Book.

Hebrews 11:1 & 6 AMP
NOW FAITH is the assurance (the confirmation, the title deed) of the things [we] hope for, being the proof of things [we] do not see and the conviction of their reality [faith perceiving as real fact what is not revealed to the senses]. 6 But without faith it is impossible to please and be satisfactory to Him. For whoever would come near to God must [necessarily] believe that God exists and that He is the rewarder of those who earnestly and diligently seek Him [out].

Heb 12:11-12 AMP
11 For the time being no discipline brings joy, but seems grievous and painful; but afterwards it yields a peaceable fruit of righteousness to those who have been trained by it [a harvest of fruit which consists in righteousness—in conformity to God's will in purpose, thought, and action, resulting in right living and right standing with God]. 12 So then, brace up and reinvigorate and set right your slackened and weakened and drooping hands and strengthen your feeble and palsied and tottering knees,

Hebrews 13:15 KJV
By him therefore let us offer the sacrifice of praise to God continually, that is, the fruit of our lips giving thanks to his name.

James 1:2-5 NKJV
2 My brethren, count it all joy when you fall into various trials, 3 knowing that the testing of your faith produces patience. 4 But let patience have its perfect work, that you may be perfect and complete, lacking nothing. 5 If any of you lacks wisdom, let him ask of God, who gives to all liberally and without reproach, and it will be given to him.

Titus 3:6 NKJV
Not by works of righteousness which we have done, but according to His mercy He saved us, through the washing of regeneration and renewing of the Holy Spirit.

I Peter 3:3-5 NIV
3 Your beauty should not come from outward adornment, such as braided hair and the wearing of gold jewelry and fine clothes. 4 Instead, it should be that of your inner self, the unfading beauty of a gentle and quiet spirit, which is of great worth in God's sight. 5 For this is the way the holy women of the past who put their hope in God used to make themselves beautiful. They were submissive to their own husbands, 6 like Sarah, who obeyed Abraham and called him her master. You are her daughters if you do what is right and do not give way to fear.

I John 2:16 NASB
For all that is in the world, the lust of the flesh and the lust of the eyes and the boastful pride of life, is not from the Father, but is from the world.

I John 4:10 NKJV
In this is love, not that we loved God, but that He loved us and sent His Son *to be* the propitiation for our sins.

Revelation 21:4, NKJV
And God will wipe away every tear from their eyes; there shall be no more death, nor sorrow, nor crying. There shall be no more pain, for the former things have passed away.

Version Notations: The difference in versions reflects only the versions in which I first memorized each passage; all of these versions are excellent.

AMP – Amplified Bible
KJV – King James Version
NASB – New American Standard Bible
NIV – New International Version
NKJV – New King James Version
NLT – New Living Translation

Appendix 4
Recommended Reading

Books About Feeling Loved by God.

Alcorn, Randy C. *Heaven*. Wheaton, IL: Tyndale House, 2004. Print

Allender, Dan B. *Leading with a Limp: Take Full Advantage of Your Most Powerful Weakness*. Colorado Springs, CO: Waterbrook, 2008. Print.

Billheimer, Paul E. *Love Covers: a Biblical Design for Unity in the Body of Christ*. Fort Washington, PA: Christian Literature Crusade, 1983. Print.

Chambers, Oswald. *My Utmost for His Highest*. Uhrichsville, OH: Barbour Pub., 2008. Print.

Christenson, Evelyn. *Lord, Change Me*. Minneapolis, MN: Evelyn Christenson Ministries, 2008. Print.

Gurnall, William, and Ruthanne Garlock. *The Christian in Complete Armour*. Edinburgh: Banner of Truth Trust, 1986. Print.

Guyon, Jeanne. *Experiencing God through Prayer*. New Kensington, PA: Whitaker House, 2004. Print.

Hattaway, Paul, and Nader Kamyab. *Heavenly Man*. Elam Ministries, 2006. Print.

Johnson, Jan. *Enjoying the Presence of God: Discovering Intimacy with God in the Daily Rhythms of Life*. Colorado Springs, CO: NavPress, 1996. Print.

Jones, Laurie Beth. *The Path: Creating Your Mission Statement for Work and for Life*. New York: Hyperion, 1996. Print.

Lawrence. *The Practice of the Presence of God*. Springdale, PA.: Whitaker House, 1982. Print.

May, Gerald G. *Addiction and Grace: Love and Spirituality in the Healing of Addictions*. San Francisco, CA: HarperSanFrancisco, 2006. Print.

McVey, Steve. *Grace Walk*. Harvest House Pub, 2005. Print.

Missler, Chuck, and Nancy Missler. *The Way of Agape*. Coeur D'Alene, ID: King's High Way Ministries, 2009. Print.

Myers, Ruth. *31 Days of Praise: Enjoying God Anew*. Sisters, Or.: Multnomah, 1994. Print.

Olson, Bruce. *Bruchko*. Lake Mary, FL: Charisma House, 2006. Print.

Sheldon, Charles Monroe. *In His Steps*. Ulrichsville, OH: Barbour Pub., 2010. Print.

Books About the Personality Types.

Baron, Renee. *What Type Am I?: Discover Who You Really Are*. New York: Penguin, 1998. Print.

Chapman, Gary D. *The Five Love Languages: How to Express Heartfelt Commitment to Your Mate*. Chicago: Northfield Pub., 1995. Print.

The Flag Page with Laugh Your Way. Web. 25 Aug. 2010. <https://www.flagpagetest.com/>.

Keating, Charles J. *Who We Are Is How We Pray: Matching Personality and Spirituality*. Mystic, CT: Twenty-third Publications, 1987. Print.

LaHaye, Tim F. *Spirit-controlled Temperament*. Wheaton, IL: Tyndale House, 1994. Print.

Myers, Isabel Briggs., and Peter B. Myers. *Gifts Differing Understanding Personality Type*. Palo Alto (Ca.): Davies-Black, 1995. Print.

Penley, Janet P., and Diane Eble. *Motherstyles: Using Personality Type to Discover Your Parenting Strengths*. Cambridge, MA: Da Capo, 2006. Print.

Southard, Betty, and Marita Littauer. *Come As You Are: How Your Personality Shapes Your Relationship With God*. Print.

Stoop, David A. *Understanding Your Child's Personality: Discover Your Child's Unique Personality Type*. Wheaton, IL: Tyndale House, 1998. Print.

Tieger, Paul D., and Barbara Barron-Tieger. *The Art of Speedreading People: How to Size People up and Speak Their Language*. Boston: Little, Brown, 1999. Print.

Trent, John, Rodney Cox, and Eric Tooker. *Parenting From Your Strengths: Understanding Strengths and Valuing Differences in Your Home*. B&H Group, 2005. Print.

Wiersbe, Warren W. *Bible Personalities: a Treasury of Insights for Personal Growth and Ministry*. Grand Rapids, MI: Baker, 2005. Print.

After Words

Continue Your Friendship with Marnie at http://www.Marnie.com.

1. Request access to the "Marnie Method Memorization Tool."
2. Listen to Marnie's weekly online training program featuring strategies, shortcuts and tips for super busy women.
3. Find out when Marnie is coming to a city near you.

Share This Book with Others.

If this book has encouraged you, share it with others!

- Suggest it to your book club or reading group.
- Take a group of God-seekers through it in your home, or study it together with a women's group at work or church.
- Give a copy to your sisters, daughters or best friends as an expression of your love for them.
- Donate a copy to your local women's shelter, prison or rehabilitation center as an extension of God's love to the hurting women who find themselves there.
- Post a note on Facebook or Twitter about how the book affected you. Include a link.

- Blog about it or invite Marnie to provide a guest blog.
- Ask your local bookstore and public library to carry copies.
- Write a book review or conduct an email interview with Marnie for your church newsletter, a local paper, favorite magazine or ezine.

Watch for More Marnie Method Books.

"Feeling Loved: Connecting with God in the Minutes You Have," is the first book in the Marnie Method series for super busy women. The second is "Kitchen Shortcuts: Cost-Cutting Cuisine in the Minutes You Have." This how-to guide includes all the kitchen shortcuts Marnie uses to serve great tasting and good looking meals to thousands of guests who visit her home, restaurant and espresso café. Her strategies will save you time and money while reducing your food-related stress. Join us for the book release party in April 2011, during Informed Women's Month, at http://www.Marnie.com.

www.ingramcontent.com/pod-product-compliance
Lightning Source LLC
LaVergne TN
LVHW041618070426
835507LV00008B/322